From Dust to Diamonds

TAG Publishing, LLC
2030 S. Milam
Amarillo, TX 79109
www.TAGPublishers.com
Office (806) 373-0114
Fax (806) 373-4004
info@TAGPublishers.com

ISBN: 978-1-934606-45-2 (softcover)
ISBN: 978-1-934606-43-8 (hardcover)

First Edition

Quantity discounts are available on bulk orders.
Contact info@TAGPublishers.com for more information.

Front cover photo by R. David Guidry Sr.

From
Dust
to
Diamonds

How small entrepreneurs can grow and prosper in any economy.

David Oreck

Contents

Chapter 1: Get a Widget. 7

Chapter 2: The Innovation of Imagination 29

Chapter 3: Little Stones Will Still Slay Goliath 47

Chapter 4: Adapt or Die 69

Chapter 5: Building Your Diamond Mine. 85

Chapter 6: Learn from Everyone. 97

Chapter 7: The Lost Art of Marketing 111

Chapter 8: The Bulldog Mentality. 127

Chapter 9: Real Growth 141

Chapter 10: Success on Your Own Terms 159

David Oreck

GET A WIDGET

David Oreck

Chapter 1
Get a Widget

Many people think that to start and run a successful company, you have to first have that one big idea. The kind of idea that will revolutionize the world or the way we live. Now there have been lots of big ideas, such as the personal computer or the cell phone, but those ideas are few and far between. The interesting thing for anyone wanting to become an entrepreneur is that it is not the one big idea that makes most people successful, it is the little ones - the kind of idea or widget that improves the daily existence of the consumer and provides value for their money. It can be something as simple as a blanket with sleeves or, as in my case, an eight pound vacuum. That's not to say the big ideas aren't worth pursuing but if you stand around and wait for one, you might be waiting a very long time.

This is good news because business success comes in many forms and via many paths so you have an infinite number of opportunities to make it happen. Though many people will try to show you the 'right' way to succeed, usually they are just showing you action steps. While some steps are important, they aren't nearly as important as how you think about your customers and your business.

Learning the specific behavior of your customers, and their wants and desires, is the real key to success, but one which most entrepreneurs don't spend nearly enough time on.

I have also found the number one element in understanding your customers is learning to define them in terms of who can buy today; not tomorrow or next week. You must have a client base with a cash base. While building a brand name over time is an important element of long term success, and one that is frequently touted as the most important, the truth is that if you don't get the customer to buy today there will be no tomorrow.

As you read this book, you will notice that there are many opinions I have that are not necessarily shared by some of the educated business minds of today. The difference is that I've done it; I took a product, created a brand and made it work, while the vast majority of the 'experts' have not. I would encourage you to read these ideas and experiences with an open mind and realize that I'm not merely spouting business theory or rhetoric. I'm telling you what I did, how I did it, and how you can do it too.

Business isn't as hard as it is made out to be most of the time – but there are some very basic ideas you have to get right. If you don't thoroughly understand those basics then your business is based on faulty assumptions and you will struggle much harder than necessary.

One of the biggest misconceptions about business that people have is the idea that your widget has to be the biggest, best, most incredible item that has ever been invented. This is not true. In fact, the widget isn't all that important. Yes, you read that right. I know it may seem completely counter intuitive to what you hear or read in the news or what is taught in the big business schools – but it is the truth.

It doesn't matter if you are making the next generation car or creating a new line of women's shoes, the 'what' is unimportant. What does matter is your ability to market that product and by market, I mean educate the consumer on why they need your particular item and why it is of value to them. Then you must listen to your consumers' feedback to continue to develop a product that meets their needs.

That doesn't mean that everything will run smoothly or according to plan and that's okay too. Sometimes unintended paths make the biggest millionaires.

Years ago, Yogi Berra said, "If you come to a fork in the road, take it!" and while it is a funny line, it is also good advice. As long as you are moving forward you are making progress even if it is not the path you originally set out on. It is only when you hesitate that the progress stops and entrepreneurs these days can't hesitate.

Entrepreneurs can easily get so wrapped up in developing their product that they don't realize development is only a small part of the equation. It doesn't matter even if you do have the biggest, best thing the marketplace has ever seen. If you can't differentiate that product from the competition, the consumer won't pay for it and you will be out of business.

I get asked all the time how I 'knew' Oreck vacuums would be successful. The truth is I didn't know. I just saw an idea that came along and took the opportunities that presented themselves. It wasn't anything special or something that I thought would change the world, but then success in business isn't about creating one life altering product. Success is about working hard and sticking to the basic ideas. Sounds easy? In fact it is so simple very few entrepreneurs actually get it right. That's not to say it isn't a lot of work - of course it is.

There are times you have to wonder if you are even going in the right direction but you must have the persistence to just keep moving forward.

It is easy to look at someone who has been successful and assume that they had an edge – like a great education, rich uncle or just luck. But for most of us, including me, that is simply not the case and I think it is really important not to focus on what you don't have because so often those things aren't what make you successful anyway. I never graduated from college, didn't have family members in key positions of power and certainly didn't win the lottery. I came from an average mid-America background with a typical family, average experiences and normal life. I didn't hob nob with the rich and powerful to get ahead; and even if I had, I know that is not something that determines success. Yet many entrepreneurs these days seem to come prepared with a list of reasons (excuses) for why they may fail before they even start and this attitude is usually self-fulfilling.

Our current economy has forced many want-to-be entrepreneurs into the business world, ready or not, and I see great opportunity for those willing to learn and work hard.

It has also created an atmosphere of fear for a lot of people, as their sense of security has been shaken and I understand that fear. As a child, I experienced the Great Depression first hand and I still carry those emotions with me. Though I was young, I remember the fear and horrible circumstances many people experienced.

My family fared better than many, but people had to rely on themselves and their own industry – there was no safety net. There were no effective social programs at that time and certainly nothing on a national level.

Recent economic difficulties have shown many people that security is often an illusion. Today you may be a high flying executive, tomorrow you may be unemployed with no job prospects. This makes the perceived risk of starting your own business much less daunting than it might be or than it has been in the past.

When I started the initial process to make vacuums as a business, I was in my late thirties and already had a long career in sales. This is the same position many people find themselves in today. They have had a career, but want to own their own business. They want to put the lessons they have learned so far to use for their own success rather than to create more profit for a corporation they only work for.

They also realize that self-reliance gives them more security than depending on a job that may get downsized or eliminated in the next corporate merger.

From Dust to Diamonds

One of the reasons I'm writing this book is to encourage those entrepreneurs that not only is it possible to start a successful business at any age, but I can give you the keys to make it successful. Anyone can be in business and there are no prerequisites or 'must haves' to make the leap. You just need to be willing to learn. I didn't know everything about vacuums before I started but I gained the knowledge I needed as I went along and you can do the same with the business you want to start.

To say I've learned a thing or two about how business really works is certainly an understatement; I have learned many valuable lessons – not all of them good.

But even in the seemingly negative events there were lessons of great value that taught me very important ideas. If you keep this same perspective when challenged it can give you an advantage and shorten your learning curve just as it did for me.

As I'm writing this I'm almost 90 years old. Though I sold my interest in the company that bears my name a decade ago, I still fly my own airplanes and run multiple businesses out of my New Orleans headquarters.

You might think that the business lessons I've learned over the past seven decades don't apply anymore because the world is a very different place now. I would argue that is not true. While we live very differently and have access to information and technology that wasn't even imagined even a short few years ago, one thing hasn't changed – people.

Consumers still have the same wants, needs and desires they have always had. They want products and services that make their lives easier, more productive or that offer a better quality of life. There will be a never ending stream of new ideas that fit this requirement and so there will be business opportunities created all the time. They haven't all been thought of and they don't all require some specialized technical know-how.

Who would have thought something as simple as a blanket with sleeves would sell in the tens of millions of units and develop a cult following in the age of flashy Internet businesses?

This proves you can create a business out of almost anything if you just give the customers something they need or want – even if they don't know they need it yet. In fact, business people today have advantages that their predecessors never imagined. For example, the Internet allows you to easily communicate and access customers all over the country and world, something that would have sounded like science fiction when I started my company. But no matter the changes that have occurred over the last 70 years, every change brings new opportunity and you just have to be smart enough to see it – and then act on it.

While I see the vast array of possibility in the landscape of today's business, I also see tremendous fear of failure in many would-be entrepreneurs. This is a strange conflict in my mind. I wonder how so many can be so fearful when opportunities are everywhere. I think it shows a real shift in thought process, especially over the past 20 or 30 years.

Somewhere along the line many people have been convinced that we must do business a certain way. We have to hire Ivy League graduates, spend lots of money and have pretentious offices. We have to get lots of education, manage a bunch of employees and spend big bucks on research and development. Did I do any of these things? No. I dropped out of college to get my pilot's license in order to ferry planes to England.

This was part of our government's lend/lease program with England prior to the U.S. involvement in World War II. During the War, I was a navigator in a B29 bomber and flew missions over the Pacific to Japan. Flying was something I enjoyed and still do. Even today I still hold a commercial pilot's license and fly my own planes frequently.

When I returned from World War II as a young man, I started at entry level, at the very bottom, taking orders largely over the phone for a company just like any other young person of my day. I wasn't special and didn't have anything special that set me apart.

You don't need anything special either. I'm not saying that things like education aren't important or are unnecessary, but it is just one small factor. For example, you might hear that to sell a product you have to have sales experience, this is not true. True selling is about educating the customer, not twisting their arm. I can honestly say I had never sold anything in my life except the Saturday Evening Post when I was a kid, and those sales dried up when I ran out of relatives!

However, I have spent decades educating customers and that, in turn, has made me very successful. People still put their pants on one leg at a time and for the all the hot air people waste talking about how things have changed, people haven't. You can still start right at the bottom and learn your way up with no experience whatsoever just like I did.

There are many concepts that are vital to business success and unfortunately, most business schools – even the 'best' schools – don't teach them. In fact, too much instruction or research can actually hurt because it can give preconceived ideas of how business should be and what works in theory.

Reality is very different. Knowledge is not talent and theory is not practice. I have spoken as a guest lecturer at more than 60 universities and even received an honorary doctorate from Pace University in New York City. To me this is proof that I do have something valuable to offer the young entrepreneur based on my real world experience.

Even before the vacuum idea surfaced, I had been a sideline serial entrepreneur. I had many side businesses back in the late 1940's and 50's and though none of these businesses set the world on fire, they provided various lessons in entrepreneurship that proved invaluable down the road. I tell you this because many entrepreneurs who are eventually successful have also failed at one point or started a company and had only lackluster results. You may have tried before too, but the only real failure is giving up. Just because one idea or business didn't hit it out of the park, that doesn't mean you can't be successful.

Actually several of the ideas I had did go on to be successful, but I wasn't at the point in my career yet where I was ready to quit my day job, so I let them go. These included an early airline charter service, a master antenna business (a forerunner of cable TV) and a magazine that was a forerunner of TV Guide. One of the most interesting businesses was a mail order radio and TV electronics repair school that offered instruction exclusively in Spanish. This was quite successful and the mail order experience would come in very handy down the road.

When I was first presented with the idea for the vacuum, I was a sales executive for the RCA and Whirlpool wholesale distributor in New York.

They had the Whirlpool brand of appliances; one of those products included a vacuum. But it wasn't really selling all that well. This was in the 1960's and you have to understand that the vacuum market was ruled by huge heavy machines which were considered the biggest and best. The assumption was that it had to be heavy and bulky to be able to do a quality job. No one ran over to me and said, "We want something different!"

This is a great lesson in consumer behavior: If you go and ask customers if they want something new, they will often say no, but if you present them with a feature that makes their life easier, they will say yes. All I said was, "wouldn't you like something lighter?" Well of course they would! Many great products have their roots in this type of understanding.

When you look back at some of the great features of products we take for granted, the questions may have sounded like this:

- Wouldn't you like a car that started without a key?

- Wouldn't you like a phone you can take with you that works anywhere?

- Wouldn't you like a remote control for that TV?

- Wouldn't you like an oven that heats something in seconds rather than minutes?

- Wouldn't you like something that magically gives you directions without having to look at a map?

- Wouldn't you like to send mail to someone electronically in seconds instead of waiting by the mailbox?

It may seem silly to think that these questions even needed to be asked, but until someone asked them, the products we have now didn't exist. If you just rely on what consumers tell you they want, you will not make the leap into innovation. You have to think of something that improves what they already have rather than trying to make what they already have cheaper.

When I started to promote lightweight as a feature, consumers didn't know it was an option because they had been trained by existing companies that in order to perform, a vacuum had to be heavy. When I introduced the idea that they could have the same performance in a machine that was easier to handle it was attractive to many customers. My target market was an older, wealthier demographic and this feature was very important to them.

Never assume that people want what is currently on the market – or whatever widget you have created for that matter. Businesses have learned this lesson the hard way many times. If you think you know what consumers want, but don't ask them and then test your ideas, you may be in for a rude awakening because customers will surprise you more often than not. For years large heavy vacuums represented quality but they were hard to use so it created an opening for another product that was light and easy to use.

You have to agree that this idea was pretty simple and straightforward. The customers responded to my idea and it was obvious that the product didn't exist, so I made one. Simple. But what is hard is understanding that these customers always wanted something light and easy to handle, they just didn't know it was possible. All I did was call their attention to the possibilities and they immediately said yes. Some of the best ideas are the most obvious. Yet we have to be aware enough to see them.

As consumers we make assumptions about products all the time and the marketing done by the makers of those products plays heavily into those assumptions. Back in the day, anything lightweight or small was considered poor quality. Everything was big – vacuums, cars, furniture, you name it. It was heavy too! Over time, consumers have been educated to think light is now good and so is small. Take the idea of the computer chip. What once filled up an entire floor of a large commercial building now fits literally on the head of a pin. But this kind of shift in understanding doesn't happen overnight.

I'm offering a word of caution here because I had to reeducate consumers before my product caught on. The idea of quality was very closely associated with the weight and heft of vacuums in the 1960's so I had an uphill battle convincing consumers that my product was quality even though it was obviously easier to use. I had to take into account the consumers' preconceived ideas stemming from previous products and how they were marketed. This helped me shape a marketing plan that worked.

That didn't mean my competition just sat on the sidelines and watched. They did everything they could to discredit my machine even to the point of calling it a toy. So I went and sold my vacuums to hotels to prove it could perform day in and day out and stand up to harsh commercial conditions. For every jab, you must have a left hook - and that requires creativity.

Over many decades of learning about consumer behavior, I have come to understand that marketing is a true art form and we will talk about it much more in-depth in a later chapter, but it is something you have to consider right up front before you even make your widget available. You have to be able to differentiate and position your product well right off; otherwise you might want to reconsider introducing it at all.

By giving some careful consideration to how you will position your widget against the competition you save yourself a great deal of disappointment and can make small tweaks early on to the design to help that widget be more unique.

Early RCA ad touting the quality of their product.

David Oreck
It is Not About Price

I find it is interesting that often when a business starts to falter, they go to an 'expert' or consultant for advice on what to do. This consultant will explain to them how knowledgeable he or she is, what degrees they have received and talk of all their other knowledge-based credits and awards. Often these experts will look at that business's product and immediately tell them to cut the price leading the entrepreneur to believe that will fix all their woes.

If I have learned just one thing in over 70 years it is that price is not the answer. Price is just one component of value but is not the end all, be all.

Effective marketing is about perception of value, not price; yet messing with price can have devastating effects on the bottom line which makes me wonder why businesses do it all the time.

When I was very young, my dad managed a retail store in Duluth, Minnesota. Each week they would get in ladies' hats that were very fashionable at the time and I watched those hats being priced. Now I knew that they had paid the exact same price for each of the hats, yet the prices placed on the hats varied significantly. When I asked my dad why, his answer was, "It's not about what the hat costs; it's about what it's worth to the customer." That was one of my first lessons in the fact that price should not be the sole focus of your business.

There will always be a competitor who can make a cheaper widget than you have, or offer a less expensive service that you do. But the consumer knows that good things aren't cheap and cheap things aren't good. If they don't want or need what you are offering, then it doesn't matter if it only costs a nickel, it still won't sell.

The value to the consumer must be established for the consumer to buy and price is not the ultimate motivating factor, it is just one component.

What business is really about is differentiating your product from the competition, even if it is just a little bit, and then educating the consumer on that difference, thus creating a good perception of value.

From Dust to Diamonds

I often speak to large groups of business people and, invariably, when I announce that price absolutely doesn't matter, there is a huge sucking sound in the room as if I've uttered the unthinkable. Not because I'm incorrect, but because so many of them have based their entire marketing and business plans on price and this idea makes those plans worthless. It is a scary thing to think you've bet your whole business on a concept that isn't helping you and business people routinely spend tremendous amounts of time agonizing over price. What they should be thinking about is how to convey value.

There was a news show on recently that featured new entrepreneurs that have been very successful and one of the companies profiled was Martha's Vineyard Clothing. These two guys started out making ties that reflected the laid back lifestyle and exclusivity of Martha's Vineyard. They revealed that it costs them less than two dollars to make a tie and they net more than $35 for each one.

When the host asked about the markup the men explained that the price was a reflection of the perception of value and had nothing to do with the production cost.

Now many new entrepreneurs would think that if it costs two dollars to make the tie, then wholesaling it for $10 would be making a killing. Or they might think that if they are going to sell the tie for $40 wholesale (similar to Martha's Vineyard pricing) then they should spend at least $10 or $15 to get it made. But they would be wrong. What it costs to produce a product has absolutely nothing to do with the perception of value and ultimate price that the market will bear. Yet, if you sit in any business class when they are talking about price, you will immediately notice that the instructors spend very little time talking about perception of value but hours and hours talking about pricing models and formulas – almost all of which are based on cost. They just don't get it.

Now think about the advertising you see every day: on billboards, TV, the Internet – how much of it focuses on price? Almost all of it. Let's take something as simple as pizza for example.

Now many people consider food to be a commodity item and use that as an excuse to focus on price, but is it? No. If that were true then you would pay the same for pizza in a cardboard box and pizza in a fancy eatery – but you don't. The difference is perception of value, not the cost of the ingredients.

Not long ago I saw a series of ads for a major pizza chain where they focused on the quality of their ingredients defeating the preconceived ideas much of the public has about their product. This is smart.

They are working to raise the perceived value, not lower the price, because once you start a price war the only move you can make is to continue to lower your price to meet your competitors until one of you, or both of you, go out of business.

Marketing isn't a Dirty Word

I think that marketing has gotten a black eye in recent years mainly because so many businesses don't understand it.

They spend a lot of money and then when people don't mob the store, they assume that they have gotten no return on their investment in marketing and give up. What is really happening is that they have no idea how to market their own product and so of course their attempts fall on deaf ears.

You will notice as you progress through these pages that I spend a great deal of time talking about marketing. It is the one business concept that I feel is almost completely misunderstood, yet it is also the one idea that can make you millions if you get it right.

Marketing doesn't have to be hard, but it does have some underlying principles that must be in place for it to work. Most people think that marketing is selling, but it is not. Marketing is educating your consumers. So what's the difference? Selling involves focusing on the buying transaction (which is where price enters the picture); educating focuses on communicating with the consumer in a way that explains the benefits they will receive from your product. When you stop trying to sell and start trying to educate, the sales take care of themselves.

This is because consumer education involves the differentiation of your product from your competitors, raising the perception of value, and creating a brand that stands for something.

It is not about price or fancy logos or flashing your website across the TV screen. All of that is secondary.

I've also sat through meetings with accountants and executives who want to quantify every single dollar spent on marketing and match that up with a tangible return. I will tell you now that is an exercise in futility. Just like cost is not connected to price, marketing shouldn't be connected with how many phone calls you get the next day. Good marketing is an art and building a brand is very hard to quantify on paper. If I ask someone about a brand that they think gets a good return on their marketing dollars, they will often pick a big company like Coca-Cola because they have a brand that is recognized worldwide. What they don't think about is that it wasn't always so and, at some point, someone made the decision to build that brand and spent many dollars doing so even though at the time there wasn't necessarily a direct dollar for dollar return on the investment.

In today's world, many businesses are tied to their monthly, quarterly and yearly profit and loss statements. They don't think long term which is what is required to build a brand and a marketing presence over time. They want to be millionaires in five years – not 25 years. When I started selling vacuums there were a lot of years at first when the business operated at a loss or at barely break even. Everything that came in I spent on marketing and gradually the sales increased and became respectable. It wasn't until the late 1980's to early 1990's that it really picked up steam. Now think about that – I started in the early 1960's and while I succeeded in building a solid household brand, it took me nearly 25 years!

These days it can be done faster as information and word of mouth for products can travel the globe with one click or one tweet. But understand that it is still a building process, not a one shot deal. You have to work hard today to get today's sales, but you also have to think long term and put in place those items that are going to build over time. This will bring you success down the road as well as right now.

Commitment

Now ask yourself, how committed are you? Are you willing to work with little to no return while you build your business? I hear all the time that most business that fail do so in the first three years and I would agree with that statistic for the most part.

Of course, attached to that are literally thousands of reasons why but I can tell you that there are only two really significant reasons a business fails:

1. They didn't understand how to market.

2. They gave up.

Now notice that I didn't mention what kind of widget they had, or where they were located, or how they priced their product. Ultimately, those items are just footnotes, what really makes the difference is the understanding of how to market to your customers and being persistent.

As long as you are in business you have the option to grow, change direction, revise your strategy or create new ideas. But once you quit it is over. You have to make the decision that you are in it for the long haul and that persistence will benefit you in every single area.

Most entrepreneurs can tell you their grand vision, but when you look at how they spend their time are they really on the path to grow that vision? I believed in my product and saw the gap in the marketplace. But it took a lot of commitment to get it going and then keep it going when sales were very modest. There are ups and downs and those swings can be extreme at times, but how you face every challenge determines if your widget will succeed or fail. You can choose to learn from your mistakes and do better next time, or you can choose to focus on that failure and get nowhere. The past is the past and concentrating on past failure just distracts you from the things you can do to improve right now, today.

When a business starts to falter, you can almost see the dark clouds gathering over the entrepreneur. Instead of focusing with even more energy and determination, fear creeps in to their minds to the point they lose hope.

They may stay in business another few months or even a year, but in their own hearts and minds they have already given up.

It is not the smartest, luckiest, or richest person who succeeds. It is the one that refuses to stop too soon.

Colonel Sanders was 61 years old and broke when he decided to try and sell his secret fried chicken recipe. He approached 1109 restaurants before he found one that would give it a try and because he refused to give up, he became a household name. Now ask yourself, do you have what it takes to keep going when number 1108 says no?

David Oreck 1959

Oreck Wisdom:

Things are never as bad as they seem to the pessimist or as good as they seem to the optimist.

David Oreck

THE INNOVATION OF IMAGINATION

David Oreck

Chapter 2
The Innovation of Imagination

The best quality an entrepreneur can have is imagination. What I mean by that is the ability to think beyond what you can see or what has already been introduced into the market. It is somewhat like looking into the future and seeing how people will live, and then creating ideas that will help them. I, like many of you, have sat through my fair share of corporate and business meetings where it seems like the only word spoken is "No". No, you can't try this or no, this won't work. I've always found in interesting that there seems to be no end to those people who will tell you what you can't do or why it won't work – but when you ask them what you *can* do or what *will* work the silence is deafening. To me that means they really have no idea what will or will not work but they'd rather not try at all than try and fail.

In order to be successful, you have to be able to weed through the advice you receive and understand that we live in a world that is in large part devoid of real imagination. So when you have a spark of imagination, don't expect everyone else to jump for joy. They probably won't even recognize the opportunity and may even try their hardest to convince you that it is folly. It reminds me of the old story about Bob Hope who was asked to be one of the original investors in Disneyland.

His response was, "Who would drive out to Anaheim to go to an amusement park?" He didn't see the vision and the opportunity passed him by. Think about the world you exist in right now and have been raised in. Most of us went to school where we were taught from day one to obey the rules, not to color outside the lines and to do what we were told. While this produces an orderly classroom, it does nothing to spur our imagination. The same is true of the college environment and even the corporate environment many people eventually find themselves in today. I was lucky in that respect.

As a young man, I got a job in New York at a company that was on the leading edge of innovation at the time. RCA was one of the leaders in the development of television and was in competition with CBS to produce the ultimate color broadcast system that would be used across the country.

My experience rivaled what people have seen in the Silicon Valley companies of the 1990's and the Internet companies of today. Creativity and imagination moved so quickly it could hardly be contained – and that was the environment in consumer products in the late 1940's and early 1950's. Television had a very small presence prior to World War II. In fact, there were less than 7000 sets in the whole country – and the war put all development on hold from 1941 until late 1946.

My first job was in the RCA wholesale distributorship and they distributed RCA radios, TVs, parts and records to retail stores. It was my first job after the war and I started basically at entry level. It was a great time to be in New York as it was truly the crossroads of the world then even more so than it is now. My wife and I lived in a typical tiny apartment as newlyweds and it was perfect for what we needed. The war was over and people were positive and energetic about the future and most servicemen, like myself, were settling down and starting families. These families needed products and the age of consumerism really ramped up.

One of the first things I learned at RCA is that business doesn't flow smoothly. It jumps and starts and even goes backward frequently. I would compare it to racing a car down a winding road at 100 mph. You feel as if you are on the edge of losing control and many times it feels as if you've lost it completely. But you keep working and things eventually come together. RCA was a big company with broadcast interests, consumer product development and research into early television technology.

Former RCA president David Sarnoff was awarded the rank of Brigadier General for his communications experience during WWII and after that was known by almost everyone as General Sarnoff. I learned a great deal from this man about many areas of business and life.

Russian by birth, his demeanor and actions often earned him a reputation of being harsh and demanding, but some entrepreneurs are perceived that way because they are pushing through new territory and that takes passion and commitment. General Sarnoff was a big player in the manufacturing and early broadcasting world but he saw the potential of television early on and worked tirelessly on what would eventually be an electronic color system. He founded NBC and was among the first to manufacture television sets. In the beginning, television was only broadcast in black and white signals. In order for someone to receive color, they would have to buy a new color set, which was very expensive at the time.

Sarnoff was working on a fully electronic system that could receive both color and black and white signals as he knew that advertisers would not want to buy advertising time if they could not have access to consumers who had either type of set.

Sarnoff's version wasn't quite ready yet and in the meantime, in 1950, CBS got the FCC to approve their electromechanical technology as the one for broadcasting. Even though the General fought the ruling all the way to the Supreme Court, he had no success in getting it overturned. I remember him calling the decision by the FCC capricious as they had just made a quick decision rather than waiting for technology to catch

**David Oreck with Robert Sarnoff,
Chairman and CEO of RCA. 1971**

up. I attended some of the hearings with the General and remember riding the train back from Washington with him.

Even when faced with utter defeat, he refused to give up on his idea and that really stuck with me. He knew that he was right and he eventually won the 'color' war He continued to fund the work on an electronic system and a short two years later, only weeks after the first color television broadcast, RCA introduced a television set to the market that could receive both color and black and white signals. This quickly became the technology of choice by the consumer and the FCC approved his electronic technology for broadcast in 1953. It has been used ever since, and was one of the very rare times the FCC has ever reversed a decision.

I've thought about this series of events many times over the years as I was developing and selling my vacuums. Each time I thought I was faced with a big obstacle, I would realize it was much smaller than the obstacles faced by RCA, but General Sarnoff was imaginative and creatively found a way to overcome anything – even when the Supreme Court refused to see things his way.

When I think back on the negative rhetoric I've heard over the course of my life , things like "people won't pay more for color TV," or "no one wants a computer in their house", or "people are never going to give up their telephone land line," or "you can't sell anything on the Internet!" I realize that innovation and imagination can change every single aspect of daily life. You can never underestimate the consumer or always predict what they will or won't do. But you can educate them on your product and create value in their minds for what you have to offer.

Change is Constant

My early experiences at RCA were exciting as I got to sit in on some of the great performances of radio and early television and experienced them live. I met a lot of interesting and well known personalities but I also saw the speed at which things change. Manufacturing for television and many other appliances took off. The country was innovating in every area in the 1950's, especially in the consumer markets. Cars, automatic washing machines, televisions (and eventually microwaves as well as many other items) were almost impossible to keep in stock.

At that time, manufacturers sold their product through the use of exclusive wholesale distributors. There were RCA distributorships around the country and these supplied the various retailers in that region. Retailers were allotted a certain amount of each item and that was because supply could not meet demand. I worked in sales and dealt with some of the major retailers in New York such as Macy's, Gimbel's, and many that have faded into oblivion. At that time though, it was less about selling and more about educating the retailers on how to present the items to the public.

The function of the independent wholesale distributor was to provide service, education and support the brand in the various local areas. The distributor would buy the product, warehouse it locally, and have a 12-15% markup to retailers. Products weren't just set on shelves with a description card for consumers to read as they are today.

There were salespeople, many of whom were trained by the distributors, who knew each product inside and out and could match your desires with the right one. They were able to maintain the value and differentiation of each brand in the consumers' minds which in turn added to the overall revenue each product could command.

Then, as now, many of the retailers were challenging to work with. They wanted the cheapest price and would then often delay payment for sometimes months. It wasn't unusual for them to find some small flaw in a product and refuse to pay for the entire shipment until that one item was removed. There were many stall tactics, but for a product like a vacuum, distribution is everything and I learned early on that if you don't control your distribution, you don't control your product.

Most appliance manufacturers learned that lesson the hard way when, in the 1970's, they began bypassing the distributors and selling direct to the big box stores. I think this was unfair and unwise. Not only did it undercut the distributors, most of whom went out of business within ten years, it also eliminated the consumer education that most brands depended on to differentiate their products. That meant they basically competed on price alone which was the undoing of many a strong brand.

When was the last time you looked at televisions and thought about one brand versus the other? This is because today they are sold mostly on price rather than differentiating features that consumers know and understand. The stellar name brands that once existed in appliance manufacturing today mean almost nothing and there is virtually no service at all. Once you sell to a discounter of any kind, your brand value can evaporate almost overnight. This is why you won't ever see a high value brand like Rolex for sale at K-mart. Not only is that not their target customer market, it also puts the power in the hand of the retailers who will then dictate how much they will pay and what the terms will be and the manufacturer is stuck having to bow to their wishes from that point forward.

This scenario is exactly what has happened in appliance manufacturing. The wholesalers initially undercut their distributors to make a quick buck, but in reality they have killed themselves. Most of the major appliance manufacturers in the US have disappeared and production has moved to Asia and other countries that can produce products cheaper. Brands that once were household names are barely noticed anymore as they are available at every big box discounter around.

Where brands are concerned, you are known by the company you keep and if you allow your product to be on sold to the discounters, then the public will discount the name of your brand until it is almost nonexistent.

Retailing, or any kind of sales, will go through life cycles for each product but also for each industry. Nothing – and I emphasize NOTHING – will remain the same forever and you must think ahead and be ready for change. Those things that are hot items now, will grow, level off and eventually fall and another will take its place as that is the way of things which is why new ideas and innovations are critical.

When I was presented with the idea for the vacuum it was to take over an existing product under the RCA-Whirlpool name. Whirlpool was an absolute unknown at that time and to increase their visibility, distribution and brand association they entered into this agreement with RCA. My contract with Whirlpool was that they manufacture the product to my specifications, and then I set about selling it just as I had sold products for RCA. Sales were slow at first as I tried the traditional routes visiting major retailers and showing them the advantages of my new product, but it wasn't enough. Then a great opportunity presented itself.

I went to visit the Ozite Company. In the 1960's Ozite had come out with green indoor/outdoor carpeting that resembled grass which you probably remember as it was very popular and ended up in millions of homes across the country. It was glued straight on to cement or sub-floor and many people used it to cover their porches, sun rooms and patios. The problem was that conventional vacuums worked by sucking air up through the carpet, so they wouldn't work on this type of low profile carpet. The result was that dirt stuck like glue to this green indoor/outdoor carpet until it looked like a big ugly mess. But I knew my vacuum would clean this new type of carpet as it used a different technology than the conventional machines and worked without having to suck air through a carpet.

So I set off with my new vacuum in tow and showed up at the offices of Ozite. I hadn't been able to get an appointment so I tried to get the receptionist to let me in to see either one of the executives or at least the head of sales. No deal. She refused. But her reception area was carpeted with the new green indoor/outdoor carpet and it was filthy.

So I asked if I could show her something. She agreed - probably just to get me to go away! But I proceeded to use my vacuum to clean the whole carpet. It looked absolutely brand new.

She immediately went and got the VP of Sales. Ozite saw the potential of selling a lot more carpeting if my vacuum was around to clean it. We agreed to do a mailing to all their retailers about the vacuum and the response was tremendous. That opened my eyes to the power of taking a product direct to consumers. These consumers with

Ozite carpeting had a problem and I had a solution. There was no rule that said I had to sell to appliance retailers or distributors just because my competition did or just because that's what I was used to. When I saw a new way to get my product out there, I took it!

You would think that good vacuum sales would make Whirlpool very happy but here again, you will be faced with unexpected challenges as an entrepreneur and I certainly was in this case. Sears was one of Whirlpool's biggest customers at the time and Sears had the Kenmore brand of appliances. The head of Sears became a board member of Whirlpool. Sears insisted that Whirlpool get rid of me, not so much because my product was competing with their vacuums, but because Sears considered mail order their domain and I had entered that area. Back then if your biggest customer said jump, you said how high, and so did Whirlpool. They canceled my contract.

We eventually went to court over the issue and I won, but it went up to the Circuit Court and because of the way the previous judge had charged the jury (not due to the merits of the case) the court sent it back down to be retried. The original judge became so angry over this that he threw the case out. So I won, but it was a hollow victory and I received nothing for my time and effort but some education in the school of hard knocks. It is times like this that really test your resolve. In order to continue with what I knew was a proven winner, I had to start my company again from scratch, with a new name and new product. I decided to name the company The Oreck Corporation. The first model vacuum The Oreck Corporation created was called the Oreck XL (Xtended Life).

Dare to Think Differently

Many of the lessons, such as taking a vacuum directly to consumers via mail, may seem obvious today, but then it wasn't. There really was no direct mail marketing and the only real marketing that had been done via mail was through catalogs such as the Sears and Roebuck catalogue. It may also seem like I was daring and forward thinking but in reality I was trying to survive. When you are forced into a corner as a businessperson, that inner creativity has a chance to shine. When things are easy, you can just keep doing what you perceive to be working when in reality it may not be as effective as it could be.

As you read this, you may think that things are so different now that none of this can help you but again, you would be wrong. Most people alive today don't even remember dedicated sales people in stores or independent distributors, but they do know that any business that provides great service is so rare that they'd pay almost anything to have it. What was commonplace sixty years ago is now rare and much sought after and this spells opportunity to the entrepreneurs of today.

The only major change over the last sixty years in many types of business is that we went from the expectation of everyone offering great service to no one offering it. It happened slowly over decades as businesses trimmed down service as a way to become leaner and save money. But the consumer still wants service – that didn't change. Anytime someone approaches me after one of my speaking engagements or appearances and starts with the line "but things are different now" my response is the same. Circumstances change, people don't. Things are different, customers aren't.

You can come up with any number of infinite solutions as long as they still solve the basic problem for the customer and so it was with my early success with direct mail. At the time it was an approach that hadn't been used all that much and it allowed a direct avenue to the end consumer without any middlemen or any damage to the brand. In fact it allowed me to really educate the consumers on my brand versus the other guys.

When you are faced with obstacles, as you will be in the normal course of business, they are your chance to try something no one else has tried before or to use some existing solution in a very different way.

What I see today is a great opportunity for businesses of all shapes and sizes to capitalize on the fact that consumers still want service, and they aren't getting it from the big guys. People don't just want to be a number in your database; they want to be known as people and for you to care about their problems.

From Dust to Diamonds

Over the past six decades so much focus has been placed on the bottom line that it is easy to forget that every sale is a person and deserving of your consideration and respect. In fact, there was a recent Geico commercial that highlighted this issue when a customer's former insurance company called her by several different names and had no clue how long she'd been a customer. She was just a number to them and that tapped into how many consumers feel they are treated by big companies today. Many companies are now seizing this opportunity to compete on service and are benefiting tremendously.

The Trust Factor

As we watch major corporations and even governments deal with corruption and mismanagement on every level, how are people supposed to trust you or your product? They don't want cheap; they want good value and getting that little bit of edge over the competitors in your market has the ability to propel your business ahead of the pack. We often think that innovation and imagination happen in a sterile laboratory somewhere but it happens all around us each day. As businesses work to define their niche among all the competitors, the most successful are those that understand their consumer, and will dare to do things differently to meet the needs of consumers in a new way even if consumers don't even know they need that service or product.

For me, new ways to connect to consumers such as Facebook and Twitter are in one respect surprising, and in another, they make perfect sense.

Facebook and similar social media sites use cutting edge technology to allow people to meet and connect with one another and seems revolutionary, but it is really not. Oh the technology is great, but the ability to connect and reconnect is an age-old human need. From the Pony Express to the telegraph to the telephone, each of these technologies were embraced because we want to connect as people – not because we want to buy the latest technology.

Mark Zuckerberg wasn't trying to change the world. He was solving a problem of human connection and it has changed the world. You must keep the underlying needs of your customers uppermost in your mind as an entrepreneur and the innovation will follow, sometimes when you least expect it or think you might have failed.

A great example of this is the story of the lowly Post-It Note made popular by 3M. 3M encourages employees to experiment and innovate, and one employee was trying to make a permanent adhesive that would stick paper to anything. But he failed because paper with the adhesive he created could be lifted off and re-stuck to another surface. He made several note pads with the failed adhesive and soon the entire office was using them. Thus the Post-It Note was born. This failure became one of the most popular products the company has ever created and has made them millions, but the innovation actually came out of failure.

Innovation is everywhere but you have to keep your mind open enough to recognize the opportunities and then jump on them.

David Oreck 1938
Ad focusing on reliability of RCA televisions. This
early modular plug-in component made servicing
very fast and easy, revolutionizing television repair.

David Oreck

Oreck Wisdom:

Think about the art of the possible:
You have to go after what can be done.
Not what should be done.

David Oreck

LITTLE STONES WILL STILL SLAY GOLIATH

David Oreck

Chapter 3

Little Stones Will Still Slay Goliath

Jumping into the entrepreneurial world can be scary, especially when you know there are well-established competitors out there ready to eat your lunch. Most entrepreneurs don't have anywhere near the advantages of their competition when they first start out. The little guy is automatically way behind the big companies in areas like capital, economies of scale, distribution, and an existing customer base - but that doesn't mean you can't compete or that you don't have advantages.

As a small business you are not encumbered by big overhead or a huge labor force, and you have the ability to be agile and move quickly on new ideas. In fact, not having all of the advantages of the big guys forces you to be creative in many areas they just take for granted and don't pay much attention to, so often they never even see you coming.

Surprise can be a great weapon to help you get the jump on the Goliaths of the world and you have to remember that every big company was once a small company. There is a great story about Sam Walton that illustrates this point.

When he started out years ago with his little discount store, he considered the big bully on the block to be Sears. In the 1960's Sears was a retail powerhouse and could have easily crushed his fledgling little Wal-Mart stores if he went head to head with them. So he created a plan in which if a town had a Sears store, he wouldn't put one of this Wal-Marts there.

What happened, over time, was is that many Wal-Marts ended up in smaller cities around the country that didn't have a Sears as most metropolitan areas did. This strategy worked and Wal-Mart was largely ignored by Sears until it was way too late. Now Wal-Mart is a global power and Sears is barely hanging on. No matter how big your competition seems today, they are not invincible.

It is interesting that back in the 1960's and 70s there was even talk of breaking up Sears as they had gotten so big some viewed them as unfair competition. I occasionally hear rumors of that same kind of chatter going on about Wal-Mart now. Who knows if they will be the next behemoth to fall hard?

When I started my company back in 1963, I had very little money, no brand name recognition at all, no manufacturing facilities, no dealers and no employees. By the time I stepped aside in terms of actively running the company some forty years later, we had approximately 1,400 employees between manufacturing and retail and were competing very effectively against giants in the industry. Make note that were not just competing, but in many ways we were beating the socks off them!

By the late 1990's, Oreck was one of the most recognized brand name vacuums in the country and that didn't happen by accident; it happened because, early on, I recognized that little stones would slay my Goliaths.

Don't Fight the Bully on His Own Turf

When you look at the solid brand names today, they appear almost invincible and the brands I competed with in the 1960's looked just as formidable. I understood that if I tried to stand toe to toe with them and go blow for blow I would be hamburger. You can think of it like getting in the ring with a great like Muhammad Ali in his prime. If you tried to fight on his terms he'd kill you with one punch. The only thing you could do was run like hell or have a shotgun!

The same is true with the small entrepreneur. You don't have the money, resources, or history to get in there and start swinging away. The trick is to develop specifically targeted techniques and approaches that are different from the big guys. You can't fight the heavyweights if you're a lightweight – and believe me, I was a lightweight in the early days in every way!

The very first step every entrepreneur has to take is to figure out what makes their product unique and then focus their efforts on educating the consumer about that unique difference. One of the first unique aspects that I advertised about my product was the fact that it was lightweight, which customers had already told me was a big benefit compared to the competition. Back then vacuums were these huge hulking beasts that did more to beef up housewives' biceps than they did to clean floors easily. So it was obvious to me that the lightweight aspect of my product was a big bonus.

The problem was, my competition called my product a toy that wouldn't hold up to the rigors of regular use. That was not good, especially since my competition had the financial muscle to let everyone on earth know exactly what they thought.

It really became an issue for me because retailers and dealers then refused to sell my product as they thought it would be perceived by the public as inferior and of poor quality. I realized that if the big boys and I faced each other in the ring with me in one corner yelling "lightweight" and them yelling "poor quality" I would never get anywhere especially since their voice was much louder. So I looked for a way to debunk their argument and prove that my product could handle more than any normal household could throw at it. That's where the hotel idea came in.

Hotels clean rooms 24/7 and go through vacuums constantly as they get much more wear and tear on a daily basis than the average household vacuum does in a year. I decided that if anything could squash my competitors' argument that my product couldn't handle regular use, it was to prove it by getting hotels to use my vacuums. I sold my product to hotels by promising great customer service if the vacuums had any problems and I got numerous contracts with major hotel chains. They knew that if my product didn't do what I said, they had me there to service any issues.

Though there were very few issues early on; I stood behind my product and provided stellar service just like I promised and that made all the difference because my competition wasn't much on service. So I took that weakness and leveraged my way in the door with hotels, then advertised the fact that major recognized hotels used my product because it was so lightweight and could handle commercial use.

In my ads, I used the image of a tiny little gray haired hotel maid holding one of my eight pound vacuums over her head and it worked! The public saw that it was lightweight and believed my assertion that it was tough and dependable, which it was. That visual was enough to conquer the other guys' rhetoric.

Choose something unique about your product then create a message for your advertising that the public can visualize and remember, just like that tiny maid. No matter what your competition comes back with, you must use your creativity to overcome their noise in the mind of the consumers.

However, a word of caution is in order here. It very common when things take a little downturn for salespeople to want to start discounting or cutting corners with the truth. Customers know when they are being handed a line of worthless drivel and you never want your company associated with that. Don't oversell your product.

If you really know your customer and what they want, your product will sell itself as you educate that customer. You don't have to give them the moon, you just need to show them the value and they will bite.

As far as discounting, I would say don't do it. How do you think your customer feels if they bought your product for $500 and then a week later their neighbor bought it for $250? It basically tells them your product is really worth $250 and they just got scammed. I believe that is one reason that consumers are so antagonistic toward airlines because they know the price they are being offered for a seat on a plane isn't really the price. They will, and usually do, see it later for much cheaper. This makes airline consumers some of the angriest and most disloyal customers that exist and it is the airlines' own fault.

If you are feeling the pressure to get more sales, your mind should immediately start working on a new way to show your customers value. Don't slash your prices, because that is cutting out your ability to market in the future and reducing your cash flow. It will also drive your loyal customers out the door once they realize your product isn't as valuable as you made them believe it is. If you are going to give your product away, you don't need a marketing plan – you need a bankruptcy attorney because that is where you are headed.

Service is Key

At the same time you employ your creativity, you have to do things better than your competition and small business still has an advantage in the area of service. Back when I was starting out you could still get service in a lot of places.

There were salesmen to help you with almost every considered (or large) purchase and you could drive up to almost any gas station and have your gas pumped for you – many services that you just don't see today. You might assume that means progress, but you'd be wrong. As a consumer group, we went from a nation that expected service to cheap big box stores that provide no service whatsoever.

Think about your own experience. Do you dread going to Wal-Mart or other large retail stores? Why? I personally don't like hiking a football field to a particular department that is frequently understaffed by people who have no idea how to help me except to read a product card. I miss the personal experience of being treated like a human instead of just one of the "billions served," and I know I'm not alone.

The opportunities for the smart entrepreneur start with treating your customers just as you would like to be treated and never losing sight that they hold the financial future of your business in their hands.

You can see smaller businesses leveraging these types of advantages every day. Walgreens touts its convenient parking and short checkout lines in a direct attack on the Wal-Marts of the world. Stores like TJ Max and Homegoods run commercials about how getting out of the mall will save you money because you can buy the same brands without the mall overhead. It just goes to show that no matter how big the Goliath is that you are competing against, you can find an advantage and that is your ticket to breaking into the market and expanding your brand.

Now you have to understand that the competition is not just going to take you chiseling away at their customer base lying down. They will throw all kinds of kinks in the works. My competitors pressured distributors and dealers not to sell my product and that could easily have been the end of me. But I had already seen the power of direct mail and continued to build upon the idea of reaching out directly to the consumer. Since I controlled my distribution, their efforts did not destroy me.

If you don't control your distribution you will be controlled by your distribution as they are in charge. Not using distributors made my company stronger as my sales were direct and not dependent on their dealer network. Eventually I started a few of my own retail stores that sold Oreck exclusively and they were very successful.

If you have a product, you can expect that your competition will try to offer something new to maintain their market share. As I was just getting a foothold in the market, my competition came up with an idea called 'tools on board' which you still see in vacuums today. The idea was that now the big hulking vacuums could clean everything from stairs to curtains with the attachments that came housed in the vacuum. This presented me with a big issue. I had looked into adding the tools on board idea, but the cost of just creating the molds to add those items to my basic design was way beyond my budget and it went directly against one of the key benefits of my product because it added extra weight and bulk. But I still had to figure out how to compete against this new offering.

My team and I spent many a night tossing around ideas to try and combat this move but our options were very limited because our pockets just weren't that deep.

That turned out to be a good thing because it forced us to come up with something creative rather than just sinking a bunch of money into manufacturing costs that we couldn't afford. We had a very small canister vacuum at the time that was just four pounds and I realized that it would be much more cost effective to add that to our package for free rather than retool our whole design for our main vacuum. As we started thinking about this idea – offering two vacuums for the price of one – I realized it actually gave us even more benefits.

The competition had taken what we saw as a weakness (the huge bulk of their machine) and added to it making it even harder to use. If someone wanted to use the tools, they had to basically dismantle the thing to get the attachments on and then drag around that heavy vacuum to clean things. Anyone who has tried to clean a set of stairs in this way knows it is almost impossible. It just wasn't practical for most users.

However, the additional introduction of our little four pound canister vacuum allowed users to go anywhere. It could even be picked up and easily carried to do stairs, curtains, furniture – whatever needed to be cleaned.

Once again, we had a hit on our hands. We made the offer for people to try our vacuums out and if the customer didn't like them, they received a free gift for trying them. This gift was usually something like a cord free steam iron that was theirs to keep whether they kept the vacuums or not. This presented the customer with a no-risk guarantee that they not only wouldn't be out any money if they didn't like our product, they would gain something for their time and trouble. This got many of them to try us out and our sales grew. This is proof you don't have to do what the competition is doing to beat them at their own game.

David Oreck
Everyone Loses at Tit for Tat

Copycat marketing is rampant these days. You see your competition offer a new product or option and so you do the exact same thing. This often just eats up your profit margin and confuses your consumers because you are no longer focusing on what makes you unique. Instead you are becoming exactly the same as your competition. Many manufacturers do this which is why you will see a new feature on one car or washing machine and six months later they all have it – even if it is not a feature the public really likes or wants. It is never good to follow the competition around rather than leading. In so doing, you have increased your costs and complexity and have not made a better or more competitive product.

I like to call this approach "me too" marketing and it just doesn't work. Instead, I think it is much wiser to use your competitor's features against them. This keeps you from adding more cost to your product while also pointing out the unique advantage you have over their offering. We used this exact approach when our competitors started coming out with bagless machines.

Our competitive position was that our bags used multiple layers of filtration and so our machines filtered the air before returning it to the room. Our bags filtered 12 times better than our competition so we used this as an advantage and focused on the fact that our machine was great for those with allergies.

Instead of following the new trend and going bagless, I stuck to the bag because I felt it represented a unique value to the consumer. With any vacuum, you have to exhaust as much air as you take in, but bagless machines allow dirty air to escape and all that dirty air can really aggravate allergies. Our bag also has a little door that seals it instantly when removed from the machine.

This is proof that a presumed advantage of your competitor can actually be creating a problem for consumers when you already have the solution. It is so important not to get in the rut of following along just because it seems all your competitors are. No one wins a game of tit for tat in business.

From Dust to Diamonds
Advertising is Education

As I have already pointed out, one of the most misunderstood, and misused, areas of business is marketing. Entrepreneurs often see marketing as a pit that swallows up their money and gives little return almost like a financial black hole. But this is because they don't really understand how marketing works or how advertising affects their long term viability as a business.

The first thing that must be understood is that marketing and advertising are different beasts. Marketing is the overall message you are trying to convey – your benefits, your brand, what you stand for as a company. Advertising is how your get that message out via print, radio, TV or Internet. You may have a great message, but unless people know about it, you are sunk. Conversely, if you do lots of advertising but the message is just drivel that amounts to clutter in the mind of the public, you are wasting your time and money. It never fails that bookkeepers often think advertising in a waste of money but I say, skimp in places that cost you money, such as accountants, and splurge in places that make you money, such as advertising.

Your challenge is to translate the knowledge you have about your product and your business into advertising that educates people about the unique attributes of your product and builds your market – and that takes time, effort, and money. One of the fallacies that many business people have is that the public always knows what they want. This isn't true.

Who wanted an oven that cooks in seconds until someone came up with it and marketed it? The public is not the originator of these ideas, but they do know when they see something that will benefit them and make their lives easier. That education is part of your job as a business person.

The first question many people ask is, "Well, that's great but where do I get the money to do all this 'educating' of the public?" The answer is that you have to build an advertising budget into your price right from the start. That's what I did. My vacuums were not the cheapest on the market and part of the reason is that when I started out I built into my price an amount that would allow me to market my product effectively and educate the consumer.

Remember when we talked about the fact that price is not the ultimate determining factor in a considered purchase? Consumers aren't all about cheap; they want value and if you price your product to include marketing from the outset, then you are giving yourself the opportunity to continually grow your market. Consumers want you to prove that you are worth more and if you do, they will happily pay the amount we would ask. Price is not the issue or everyone would buy everything generic and we would all drive beat up used cars. You have to prove your worth and always remember that value sells product,not price.

For most of the first ten years almost all the profit that came into my business I reinvested in marketing because I know how powerful it can be. I felt that every dollar I invested had the potential to grow the market and brand. I focused on direct mailings that reached the consumer right in their home and this had a couple of great benefits. First, it allowed me to educate them without the distraction of a bunch of other advertising they were used to seeing and hearing as there was very little junk mail in those days. They could read my direct mail piece and focus on the message I was conveying. You also have to remember that at that time there really weren't any vacuum companies reaching out to the consumer directly by mail so my marketing was unusual and that's important.

I could identify the customer, the area of country, whether they were male or female, income, marital status, age and any number of demographic groupings. The cost of advertising is so high you can't afford to pay for ads to people that are not your target market. If you have a premium product you have to have some way to prequalify the customer to get the maximum return possible and that is true whether you are spending $500 per month or $50,000.

In the case of Oreck vacuums, I targeted an older demographic because I wanted to sell to someone who had more disposable income and to whom a lightweight machine would appeal. I specifically targeted those most likely to appreciate the benefits of my machine and thus received as large a return on my advertising investment as possible.

From Dust to Diamonds

For whatever reason, many businesses erroneously focus on capturing a 'young' market. I'm not sure exactly why they want to attract this base of consumer but in my case, it made absolutely no sense.

They don't have the disposable income to purchase a vacuum such as mine, nor do they have the same concerns with the machine being lightweight. That's why I used a gray haired maid in some of my early advertising. I wanted customers to identify with someone in their own age group because that was my target market. It is interesting that even at the time, there were advertising people who thought I should use a beautiful svelte young model in my ad, but that seemed ridiculous to me and it turned out I was right.

At that time, my competitors all had advertising that showed young beautiful woman using their product, but it was not right for me. This goes back to the idea that you don't want to go up against the competition on their home turf. I couldn't buy more print ads or radio time than they could; I was just the little guy and I could easily be drowned out. But I could create a very unique and different message and use the most creative ways possible to get that message to the consumer.

These days some of the most creative advertising you see is on infomercials and they have the right idea. It is not just a commercial because they are conveying information and educating the consumer. They take the time to show demonstrations, give testimonials, and make you an offer you just can't refuse.

That is what good advertising does and you know it works when you see a spot for a new type of fish hook and consider buying it even though you don't fish! I think that it is a good idea to watch some of the more successful commercials and infomercials and take notice of what really gets your attention so you can emulate that same tone and type of offering for your own product or service.

If it gets your attention, then it is getting the public's attention and that's a good indicator of someone doing things right. It is important to understand that educating the customer isn't about hucksterism, its educating people that there's a better way and easier way to do something. It is also not about showing how great you are, or what kind of award winning ad you can make. Customers will not care until they know what's in it for them.

Advertising is crucial to your business' growth and in order to do it well, you must be able to present a story that is credible and attractive to the consumer while showing them what is in it for them. For example, my story was all about ease of use.

The bottom line is that the consumer doesn't really care who you are or what you do – they want to know how you can help them and that has to be the story you tell. I focused on how easily you could clean your rugs with my lightweight vacuum. It is not a complicated or hard story to tell but it was about making life easier and who isn't interested in that?

Part of the story you tell can, and should, include service and some kind of guarantee to lower the risk for the consumer. I offered stellar service with a 21 year guarantee. I also offered two vacuums for the price of one with a free gift so there was little risk. Part of the 21 year guarantee was based on the fact that the customer brought the vacuum in each year for a tune up. For the customer this was like insurance that their machine would last for years, but what it was really about was giving the dealer a chance to reconnect with that customer at very low cost - much less cost than running any advertising. During these visits, we put their machines back in perfect working condition at no cost to the consumer.

We'd replace the belts and whatever needed to be done, but while the customer was there, we'd ask if they've seen the new rug shampooer or air purifier. It was a way to bring the customer back into the store to get a free tune up and gave the dealer an opportunity to show them the new products. It was a perfect idea that didn't cost the dealer anything since the cleaning and tune up often just took minutes. It was a good formula.

Now think about today. If a customer buys something from Wal-Mart, who do they see for service? The cashier? The ability to connect and give excellent service allows that good emotion to transfer to your product. People to this day will say they love their Oreck vacuum.

From Dust to Diamonds

Oreck ad 2008
This ad shows the power of a guarantee.

This is not because we have the only vacuum out there, which is obviously not the case, but because our product delivers on its promise to make their lives easier and because there are people behind the product who know how to treat customers. Any customer who said up front that they wouldn't bring their machine in for yearly service, I would say we're not for you and you're not for us. It was never worth making a sale to have someone be disappointed down the road. What we did with Oreck was fantastic because it was something that hadn't been done before in terms of marketing a product direct to consumers.

Though we were much smaller than the big guys, tiny in fact in terms of total sales, may people assumed that we were the #1 vacuum cleaner company. This is because we acted like we were the best and we were in terms of service to the customer. Even today, decades later, Oreck is frequently thought of as the #1 vacuum cleaner and many of the vacuums that have surpassed that original 21 year guarantee are still going strong.

Virtually every other vacuum manufacturer is now owned by the Chinese including Hoover. Most other smaller companies have gone out of business. If ever there was a classic case for what to do as a little guy getting started, we are good example of that and it wasn't because of a unique revolutionary new design or earth shattering product. Vacuums haven't changed a heck of a lot since the 1900s. Yes, we've added features, but nothing revolutionary. Our success was in creating a story that people could really relate to and getting that story out through effective advertising.

The Tail Wags the Dog

Advertising is another area of business where what they teach in business school isn't really what needs to take place in real life. You've all seen those ads that are all artsy and confusing to the point you have no clue what the product even is. Those ads tend to win advertising awards, but they don't sell product. You are in business to sell product. You can't afford some art piece that drains all your cash and gets you no customers.

From Dust to Diamonds

Let's think about the advertising we see today. Everything is the biggest and best, or it slices, dices, cuts through beer cans and feeds your dog. There is almost no claim a manufacturer won't make and this has created a consumer that is more skeptical than ever. I've heard it said that today most of us are bombarded with up to 10,000 messages per day and with that kind of noise, who is the consumer to believe?

You must stand out and I'm a big supporter of having a good spokesperson. I've been the spokesperson for Oreck on all our advertising. Now this is not because I have that 'male model' kind of face! In fact, I'm pretty ordinary looking and that is one of my strengths. I am an average Joe with a great product that I really believe in and you can't trade anything for that.

Oh you can get some eye candy and have some sweet young thing showing off my vacuums but who is the public going to believe more? They'd probably watch that ad and wonder if she's ever vacuumed in her life. But when they see me on the screen, they know I love my product and I can help them.

Advertising people will sometimes give you advice that sounds good but in reality doesn't help you. I had advertising people tell me that I needed a woman to present my product because my target market was women. That's bologna! If you are a credible spokesperson for your product, then you have an advantage. People can sense your sincerity, honesty, and genuine enthusiasm. They know if you are or aren't trying to pull a fast one and sometimes if the ad looks too slick it makes them suspicious. Go with your gut and don't believe that someone else can promote your business better than you can.

I've learned a lot over the years, but I'm amazed by the number of Ivy League educated people who just don't get it. When it came to writing this book, I promised myself I wouldn't pick them apart, but they really don't understand marketing. I have to say that it is not really their fault, they just haven't been taught nor have they experienced enough to know better. They're good bookkeepers. They understand that. There's always a formula that they think applies to advertising, but it doesn't work like that. In the case of radio, which I think is a very powerful advertising medium, supposed 'experts' will try to measure the effectiveness of the ad by the number of calls you get from a radio ad vs. the cost of the ad.

Now think about that. Here's a guy driving 70 mph, a captive in his own car listening to your message on the radio. So what does he do? Does he screech to a stop on the side of the road to make a telephone call to get a free demonstration of a vacuum in his own home right then?

No, he doesn't, but he does hear the message and that is important. But then in the marketing meeting the next day, these bookkeepers or business managers, say the ad didn't work because there weren't enough calls for them to justify the cost.

Now the consumer that heard that commercial probably won't pull over and call, but later may see the ad in a magazine or on the Internet and he remembers the story you told about how that product can make life easier. He decides he likes the product.

Does that mean the radio ad had no value? No, it is just that the time line from consumer awareness to action can't be measured in a direct quantitative way. Marketing is not something you can measure easily no matter how many formulas you have. You have to have a gut feeling for what is working and what is not. If you don't get an immediate result, it doesn't mean your advertising didn't work. You have to pursue that which you believe in and hope you're right. This means educating your consumers even when they don't show up on your doorstep in droves.

Teaching people about your product is never a wasted effort and over time you will reap big rewards but only if you use all the little stones in your arsenal and chip away at the Goliaths that stand in your way.

Oreck Wisdom:

Keep prices high and margins high.
That way you can afford to advertise.

David Oreck

ADAPT OR DIE

David Oreck

Chapter 4
Adapt or Die

It is not unusual for small business to always feel like the underdog. What makes the difference is if you see your underdog status as good or bad. No doubt there are just some things you can't do that the big guys can (like throw money around) but that doesn't mean that you can't be just as effective, or even more so, when reaching customers. In all my experience both in the corporate world and as an entrepreneur, I've learned that more money doesn't equal more brains nor does it ensure your success. Does it really matter if your competition is spending millions if those millions are really wasted? No, it doesn't and in fact it helps you when the other guys don't understand some of the basic business principles just like the ones I'm sharing with you in this book. Almost everyone assumes that big companies have the best and brightest and that they know what they're doing. So often, small businesses try to emulate what bigger business do, but this is usually a big mistake.

Now don't get me wrong, big business does have the resources to attract some of the most educated people in the world. But in business, if you don't have a good understanding of your customers, and a basic understanding of how to market yourself, then that fancy degree might as well be in basket weaving.

Don't be intimidated or feel bullied into strategies that don't work simply because you feel like you have to keep up and follow step. You don't. You have to be imaginative and creative and because you are the underdog, often your competition won't even see it coming and this is a big advantage.

Small business has numerous advantages that are overlooked or devalued on a regular basis, just like the story of Sam Walton trying so hard to avoid Sears. It made Walton a powerhouse in small towns and led his company to eventually dominate the discount market. So you can't overlook any advantage you might have. For example, one of these advantages is the fact that a small business has the opportunity to change gears and exploit an opportunity at a moment's notice. There are no weeks of meetings to evaluate the idea, or approvals needed for travel or any of that other nonsense.

If I saw an opportunity, I booked a flight and went and that was that. The same is true of advertising ideas that I would have. If something popped into my head, we tried it immediately and then forced our competition to play catch up instead of the other way around. You can try creative ideas and see what works. Big business is like a huge gangly beast that takes forever to get going and once it does can't seem to change direction very easily – but you can.

The same is true if something isn't working. You have the option to stop it right then and try something else whereas your larger competitors might spend millions to find out the same thing and take months (or years) to change direction. The ability to make decisions on the spot and then quickly recover from errors is a great benefit for small business owners and one that few people really value. Every time I felt something wasn't working I could try something else and I viewed every one of these instances as learning opportunities. If I could learn faster what did, and did not, work I could move ahead of my competition and stay there. I encourage every entrepreneur to value those things that may seem like mistakes or errors and learn the lessons they are teaching you.

From Dust to Diamonds

Today's market is very fast paced and you have to be fast paced as well to stay ahead, but that doesn't mean running around in a panic. It means you must watch for those opportunities and when they show themselves, be ready to pounce.

You can't stand around in an indecisive haze just because you are afraid to make a mistake. Every misstep along the way is just priming you for greater success down the road so set that fear aside and leap out into the fray.

Think About Your Customer

One of the things that big business rarely does is to really think about their customer - who they are, what they look like, how they live, or what really matters to them, but this is something that the entrepreneur must do. You have to know your customer. You have to slice 'em, dice 'em and know everything about them inside and out. This is because it all comes down to money. You don't have an unlimited budget to reach people, so you can't spend on those who are not in a position and likely to buy today. You have to focus.

I can't tell you how many business people I have talked to, when asked who their customer is, says "Everyone."

Your customer is not everyone and it doesn't matter what product you have, no product will interest every single person. Think about this: if you make mousetraps who are your customers? The answer is not everyone. Your customers are people who have mice and want to get rid of them. If you make a lawn mower who is your customer? Again, not everyone, just those people who have lawns and want to cut them themselves. Do you see how this narrows things down to your real customers and allows you to start targeting those who will actually buy your product?

Targeting your consumer is one of the most important and cost effective things you will ever do. Millions of dollars are spent every day on marketing that is being used like a scatter gun and just aiming at whomever happens to see it rather than those who might actually buy. I used this idea of really defining my customer to narrow down the target market for my product based on the features it offered. You cannot afford to advertise to people who cannot afford, or who are unlikely to buy, your product. For example, feminine hygiene products would not be advertised in a men's magazine, nor would they be advertised in a magazine focusing on retired people. You must identify much more closely the target market. Even down to the smallest things. From the general region they live in, down to the part of town or zip code.

For example if you have a swimming pool product, you have to target those with swimming pools otherwise your message falls on deaf ears and is money wasted. You may think that there is not much difference in consumers who buy a common household item such as vacuums but you'd be wrong. I really spent a lot of time thinking about the kind of person that would be the most likely to buy an Oreck vacuum – not just any old vacuum. The first thing I considered was the fact that it was lightweight. Now this probably wouldn't be that big a feature to someone in their twenties who had no problem hefting a vacuum up stairs or all around the house but their mother would take notice of a vacuum that weighed only eight pounds.

Consumers from about age 35 on up want something that requires less upper body strength so right away, I narrowed my target market to those over age 35 and even more specifically, the 40-65 age range. This age group was also a growing population with the Baby Boomers so my market would grow over time (and it certainly has).

My product was also more expensive than some others on the market and I worked hard to build value into my brand, but it was a premium brand so I knew right up front that not everyone could afford it. This meant that my customer had to have a good income so that allowed me to narrow the idea of my customer even further. Then I thought about the fact that women buy most of the vacuums that are sold.

Even in today's more forward thinking world, women still do most of the vacuuming at home and they make the vast majority of vacuum purchases. So I decided that my customer was most likely a women

Oreck Hotel Maid ad
This ad highlighted the lightweight feature of Oreck vacuums while also showing they could stand up to commercial use.

between the ages of 40 and 65 who lived in a relatively affluent area. In my mind, she was a gray-haired grandmother much like the image of the hotel maid I used in my ads.

By using direct mail to target these customers, my advertising went right to the people who would possibly buy my product and wasn't wasted on the public at large. By taking the time and energy to really think about my customer I could also develop advertising that really appealed to them and spoke directly to their concerns.

Every time I thought about a new product or new advertising I always had a visual image of this customer in my mind and asked myself, "What would this person think?" Taking the time to really consider who your customers are saves you time and effort in the long run and keeps you from straying too far from what would please those customers. The customer wants to know, what is in it for me? Put yourself in their position.

Today especially, you see big business trying to figure out if their product and advertising is appealing to what they consider to be their target market. One of the most popular ways they do this is with focus groups.

Focus groups are a few people (usually 10 to 50 depending on the product) that fit the description of their target market as far as age, income, and various other criteria, that come together and give their opinions. But in my opinion, I think these groups are worthless. Results from focus groups, like anything else, can be made to confirm exactly what you want them to confirm no matter what it is. Much like telephone polls can show almost any result depending on how the questions are phrased.

It is very easy to lead the witness, so to speak, and that means the information gathered is of no real value. Focus groups also waste a great deal of time and money that could be spent on test marketing which has much more validity. Focus groups will allow you to get the answer you want because they will tell you what you want to hear. But getting the answer you wanted in the first place will not help.

From Dust to Diamonds

When you ask a person who is not an expert to evaluate a product or some advertising, it is like asking a blind person to describe the color blue. Since they have no idea the context in which you will be using the information, they can offer little but their own limited opinion which is usually completely off base. For example, if you ask a woman on the street what appeals to women, how can she really answer that?

All she can tell you is what might (and I stress *might*) appeal to her. Once you ask someone for an opinion, they often come up with all sorts of things that they normally wouldn't have thought of that are more or less meaningless because you have pressed them for some kind of answer.

This idea is true even of the experts. If you ask an 'expert' for their opinion I guarantee they will have one but it may be completely useless. Some of you may have had the experience of running a simple contract past an attorney. If you have done this, then you also know that there is no contract that is ever good enough or that an attorney won't pick apart when asked for an opinion. Does this mean the contract is bad? No. It means you asked for an opinion and he has to find something to justify his status as 'expert' even though the contract may be great.

The same is true with advertising. If you put your ad in front of a big advertising executive and ask for an opinion they will usually tell you how it needs to be changed and why it won't work. But that doesn't mean your ad is bad – in fact it may be better than anything their marketing people can produce.

I was told by many an advertising expert that what I was doing marketing wise was wrong. All I can say is that it worked great so how wrong could it have been? I say this because often much of the 'expert' advice is tainted by self interest. Advertising people sell their services, not your product, and you must remember that. If your ads are working and they can't convince you to use theirs instead, they have nothing to sell you and can't get your business. Listen to those who have been successful doing what you want to do rather than a bunch of experts, because those business people have hands on experience and know what works.

David Oreck
Uncommon Sense

Many of the ideas I'm sharing with you may seem like common sense and they are, but the idea of common sense is really an oxymoron. If it were really common then everyone would do it. It is really uncommon sense that will make you successful. You need only to look around and see the truth of this in action every day. Have you ever seen something ridiculous that a smart, well thought of business person did and wondered, "What were they thinking?" This happened to me during the recent economic down turn as the big car companies faltered. I saw on the news that the head of General Motors was heading to Congress with a tin cup to try and get a government bailout – in a $50 million dollar jet! What was he thinking?

Common sense would have told him to drive a Chevy but his habit was to fly around in the expensive jet which revealed a lot more about the problems at GM than his testimony before Congress did.

He wasn't running the business like an entrepreneur would have; he was running the business as it had always been run during the good times and was unable to redirect his efforts when things got tight. This type of thing happens all the time and proves that the little guy may be unsophisticated, and he may not have an Ivy League education, but he can choose to be smart and creative and that counts for a lot because big business can make catastrophic mistakes.

Uncommon sense will also tell you that price is not the answer to everything. Uncommon sense will tell you that people want value. Uncommon sense will tell you that you must educate your customer. Keep those ideas in mind as you build up your product in the mind of your consumers. Not everyone drives an old beat up used car because consumers don't just want cheap; they want quality and are willing to pay for it. If you have a premium product you have to explain to the consumer why it is a premium product and how it will make their life better. One of the ways you do this is by shifting the customer's perspective.

Now if someone said a car was going to cost me $20,000 I would think that is a lot of money because no one has put that price into context for me or given me a perspective that makes sense. But if the salesman said it was a year old Lexus, and that a brand new Lexus costs $40,000, I would suddenly think that was a great deal! This is the type of value perspective you must give the customer. If my product is $299 and a similar product is $69, then I have to give the customer a reason for the difference.

One of the ways I did this with my product was to offer the 21 year guarantee. Then my salesman could tell the consumer 'you will never have to buy another vacuum'. Of course the consumer immediately does some cursory math in their head and realizes this product will actually save them money in the long run so suddenly my product seems valuable and the competitor's product seems like a throw away item.

You see this all the time in advertising from high end retailers like Tiffany's. They don't splash a price across the ad – in fact you have to hunt for it in the fine print if it even appears at all. That's because they know that price doesn't matter.

They have a premium product and their advertising is teaching you all about the stones and quality workmanship of their jewelry. You will see something similar in Mercedes Benz commercials. They spend the whole commercial talking about how it feels to drive the best and how others will perceive you when they see you driving that kind of premium car. Price is just an afterthought.

This idea translates to every single product. Even the simplest product can have value added and be differentiated from the competition whether that be a fancy mouse trap or a pair of blue jeans.

Perfection is Highly Overrated

It can be hard sometimes to tell the difference between something that isn't working and something that just needs more time. It may sound a little fuzzy but the best advice I can give you in this case is to trust your gut. If you have truly considered your specific target customer, and you are spending your dollars to reach out to them in the most creative way you know, then sometimes it is just the message that needs tweaking in order for the revenue to really start flowing in. Don't expect to get it right the first time. Commit to the idea that you are going to have to keep trying.

One of the most detrimental attitudes that I see among entrepreneurs is when something gets no response, or mediocre results, they go right to 'quit' rather than trying to tweak the message to get better results. No one hits it out of the park on the first try. Marketing can be frustrating which is why so many experts try to make it a science and come up with the perfect formula. But it is not a science; it is an art, and that takes time, patience and practice to perfect.

I often hear business people talk about how they 'tried' TV and it didn't work. Or they 'tried' radio and it didn't work. How do you 'try' an advertising medium and then just throw in the towel? Every channel of advertising from the Internet to billboards has some value but you have to figure out the right message for each avenue and which ones work for your product. You don't just toss out the whole medium just because the one ad you ran for a week didn't get you thousands of phone calls.

You have to work hard to refine your message and then push it through the right targeted medium. There is an old saying that I have found to be true and that is the fact that you can bring more pressure to bear on the point of a pin rather than over a broader surface. If you find one point that is a good one you strongly emphasis it even if you exclude other points. You can't be all things to all people. You have to pick that one defining idea and push it hard.

When something is difficult, or takes time effort and money, it is human nature to want to push it aside and blame everyone and everything else. But if you want to be really successful you will choose to take on the responsibility to learn. You won't blame TV or radio en mass, or your advertising firm (if you have one). You know the unique benefits of your product and how to sell it or you wouldn't be in business. Stick to that knowledge and then learn to translate that in a way that reaches people even if it takes a lot of testing and a lot of failure.

Early on, some of the ads I did were not very effective, but I tried various approaches and when I found one that worked, I honed it over time to make it even better. It was a process. I didn't get to 'perfect' on day one and that's still true today. While I certainly have the benefit of decades of knowledge and have a much better starting point than I did way back when, I still have to work at narrowing down the message depending on the product. So don't be too hard on yourself or think that you have to get it right the first time. Just know you must keep trying because the only time you really fail is when you quit.

As you evaluate what you are currently doing to market your small business, revel in the idea that you are the underdog and leverage the advantage you have right now to become an iron-fisted competitor. You are not using financial status as a measuring stick because you are competing for the hearts and minds of the customers first and foremost and their dollars will follow.

Even now, more than ten years since I released the operational control of the Oreck company, if you ask the average person on the street to list the bestselling vacuum in the U.S., many of them will say Oreck. This isn't because we actually sell the most vacuums, we don't.

This isn't because we are the cheapest, we aren't. But I set out to win the war of perception in the minds of consumers, I worked hard and marketed my product constantly in the most creative ways possible and I won, and Oreck is still winning because of it. Score one for the underdog.

Controlling Growth

I already talked a little bit about the fact that controlling your distribution is key. But so is controlling your brand image and that means who your brand associates with. The brands that are the lowest cost are not the brands that you find in the most exclusive retailers and vice versa.

Inevitably when I speak to groups on college campuses, there is at least one person who believes that to really succeed, then they must develop a product and sell it to Wal-Mart. This is the opposite of success. Once you sell to a big discounter you are handing over your product and they will then dictate what you will or will not do. If you don't bow to their wishes they can, and will, put you out of business in a heartbeat, end of story.

But there is an exception to that rule and that is when you have grown your brand to the point that you have control rather than the retailer. Recently I saw a great example of this and that was a deal that was completed by Martha Stewart. No matter what you may think of her personally, Martha Stewart is an astute business person. She has literally spent decades protecting her brand and ensuring that it was associated with quality. So much so that she currently has an exclusive deal with Macy's to market her top of the line home products.

She knows her market and she knows what appeals to that demographic and has become the biggest home wares brand that Macy's sells. Recently JC Penny bought a 14% stake in Martha Stewart and that company will now begin to market some of her lines as well under the Martha Stewart brand.

This might seem like suicide because Macy's could tell her to go jump in a lake, but in this case it was very smart and here's why. Martha Stewart did the exclusive deal with Macy's but it was dependent on her having control of the product.

She had built the company brand image over time so much so that she had the power, not the retailer, and Macy's agreed to the arrangement ensuring her control of the product.

Once she became the leading brand in the home wares division of Macy's she knew that she was safe to then make deals with other companies. She was safe because she knew Macy's wouldn't (and couldn't) drop her bestselling brand right away without hurting their bottom line tremendously.

She then used that leverage to move into other markets while all the time maintaining control of her product and her brand. Now I have no idea if this will work in her favor, but I see it as someone who is trying to use the power of the brand they built to widen their business. There is always a danger of pitting competitors against each other with your brand in the middle, but if your brand is big enough you can make it work for you.

Waiting until you have built a strong brand to work with major retailers is an idea that many small entrepreneurs don't understand. You must stand alone first and be a strong contender in the marketplace before even considering going into a large discount retailer. This allows you to set terms and control your product. Otherwise the brand and product will be diluted to the point it is meaningless and soon you will be replaced by similar, cheaper products from China or elsewhere. Small entrepreneurs must learn to say no to the big discounters early on in order to preserve their future, but few are able to do so because the lure of that big contract is so enticing.

I kept to my marketing direct to consumers and that grew my brand. It meant something to consumers and I never chose to dilute that brand by selling to the Wal-Marts of the world. Sure it was hard, but what part of owning a small business isn't? In the end, it grew exactly how I wanted, in the time I wanted by preserving that which made my product different and unique, which was the real value.

David Oreck

Oreck Wisdom:

You must stand on your own two feet first and build your brand, otherwise you will be crushed by big retail in a heartbeat.

David Oreck

5

BUILDING YOUR DIAMOND MINE

David Oreck

Chapter 5
Building Your Diamond Mine

When you make the decision to go into business for yourself, you have to think of it as your own personal diamond mine. You start with nothing and then hack and blast away all the things you don't want in order to get to the precious stone underneath. Building a business is just that – a building process. You don't just decide to be a business person one day and then instantly it happens. But more and more I see entrepreneurs who want this sort of instant gratification and they will trade almost anything to get it, only to regret it down the road.

When the Oreck Company first started out it was a bare bones operation and that was a key element to its eventual success. I see many new business people who start out first with the big impressive office. Then they hire a bunch of staff so they feel like they are 'in business'. Most of the time that's a mistake because you can accomplish much more in a shorter period of time if you don't strap yourself to loads of overhead. I didn't need an office to sell my vacuum. I traveled around and presented it to various distributors then when I discovered the power of direct mail, we sold through that avenue. For a long time we stored product in an old semi-trailer. I had a very simple office and minimal staff – and it worked.

I think people often take on overhead and unnecessary expense to try and impress others or their customers. If you have a great product that works and meets their needs, none of that is necessary.

Of course it depends on the type of business you have. If you own a restaurant or retail shop then a slightly different business model is in order, but the idea that you keep your overhead as low as possible is still valid no matter the type of business. You only want to add staff and amenities as they become absolutely necessary, not just because they are convenient or because you want to spend more time on the golf course.

This brings up another myth that I think many would-be entrepreneurs tend to buy in to and that is the idea that they can get the business started and then step away and pay someone else to run it. These type of people like the idea of being a business owner but aren't willing to put in the dedication and hard work it takes to really make it successful. Being in business is hard work and you simply can't pay someone else to care.

They will be happy to do their job, punch the clock and go home but they will never have the vision or desire to make the business as big a success as you will. It is easy to look at someone who has spent years building a business and who has a great management team in place and assume that you can do that too. Of course you can over time, but not instantly and what you don't see are all the years of sacrifice and work on the front lines that it took that business owner to get to that point.

Warren Buffet often says, "No one washes a rental car." What he means is that without a proprietary interest in the business, no matter who you hire they will never treat your business as well as you do. While it may be tempting to not share what little wealth you have with employees, if you loosen your grip and give them a proprietary interest (even a very small one) they will work harder, longer for you than they ever would have otherwise. You want to be the head guy who gets to take off on vacation knowing the business is taken care of instead of the business owner who stays home and worries while his employees take off and enjoy life.

Own Your Own Destiny

When you sit and think about all the shortcuts you possibly can take to business success, one of the first things that comes to mind for most people is the idea of taking on a partner.

On the surface it seems like a good idea because you can spread the work and the risk beyond just yourself.

I will tell you that over the last 70 years, I've seen very few partnerships that have been more than dysfunctional disasters. Just as it is extremely hard to find a spouse you can live with as a spouse for decades, it is even harder to find a business person who you can work with for that long and be productive. They almost always end in a split of some sort that either completely destroys all they have worked for or leaves the business in on life support.

While it is hard sometimes to go it on your own, someone has to have the last word if you are to move forward effectively. Taking on partners is like running a business by committee which causes unnecessary delays and gives mediocre results at best. That's not to say that you don't listen to the advice or counsel of others, especially those more experienced than you. Take the advice you can get but then make the decisions yourself. While it is true you will make mistakes, they are your mistakes and that is much easier to live with then having to put up with the mistakes of someone else, especially when the business is on the line.

Another way I see some entrepreneurs trying to take a quick shortcut is to find venture capitalists or investors to fund their idea. Now I'm not going to beat up on investors but I will warn you that it is hard to make good decisions when you are constantly being second guessed. It can be difficult to create the personal confidence necessary to make the hard decisions in business and investors, silent partners and venture capitalists can undermine that confidence very quickly. Why have your own business if you still feel like you are working for someone else?

Here again, I'd like to offer some reassurance that you are smarter than you think you are. If you really grasp the ideas of marketing and advertising in this book you are way ahead of 99% of business people and this includes investors. It can be easy to think that they know more than you since they have made money and you haven't yet. They may have fancy degrees and know all kinds of business details that you aren't really familiar with. It can be logical to assume they are the experts but more often than not, they have no idea how to make a business successful. More than once I've seen investors come into a company and right off the bat change the advertising and marketing.

Inevitably they make the same mistakes that I've already talked about by competing on price rather than understanding how to add value. When revenues fall, they often will blame the entrepreneur, not their own faulty assumptions. So don't think for a minute you can't own and run your own business. You can, you just have to work hard at building it and then be patient while it gains momentum.

And Then There's Family . . .

Many small businesses are run by family members. Often this is out of necessity more than anything. Family tends to work cheap and put up with more than the average person off the street and there is already a relationship and trust factor going on. But family can be problematic. Now it is true that I've worked my company with the help of my brother Marshall for over 40 years and it has worked well but I also know that is the extreme exception. When someone asks me if they should go into business with family I will always say no. Not because it hasn't worked for me, it has, but because I have seen countless other businesses destroyed by it. Not only can it destroy the business, but in the process it can also destroy the family and no business is worth the risk of losing your family relationships.

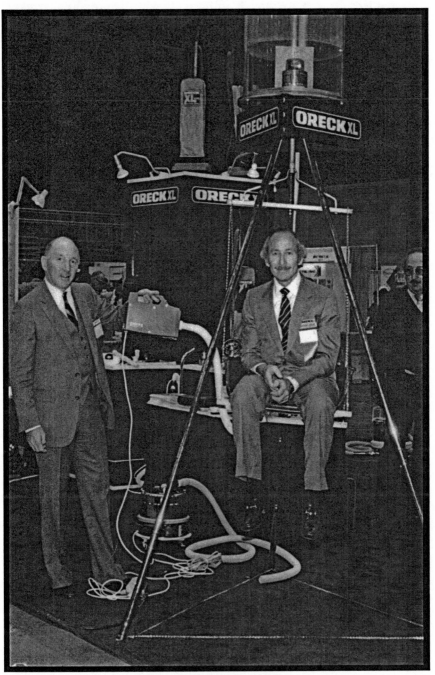

Convention Booth 1980
David Oreck and Marshall Oreck

Now let's say you are already in business with family. What works? And what makes it work better? One key distinction that has made my situation work well is that there was always a clearly defined hierarchy. I was the business owner – period. So the final decisions, and risks, were mine. The idea of who has the power is a big issue in family owned businesses and it needs to be laid out, even written down and agreed on, to function well.

Marshall and I also had our own distinct areas we focused on and that helped. I was the outside man, and he was the inside man. In other words, I traveled to promote and sell the product while he took care of fulfillment and the office. Even if you are not working with family, having clearly defined job descriptions and areas of focus can make any business run much more smoothly. As you take on more staff it is up to you as the owner to make sure you clearly define each person's area of responsibilities; you never want to just leave them to work it out.

Even before the first day you start to work with family, you should have an exit plan. What happens if there is a divorce, or unhappy spouse that thinks they deserve more of the profits? What happens if you need to fire a family member? What if they quit? It is important to discuss these ideas from the very beginning and have an understanding of the possible downfalls. Then you can create a strategy to deal with them if they ever arise, and it won't be clouded by the emotions of the moment.

Communication is one of the key factors that make a business work very effectively and with family you have to communicate much more than if they were just employees. Marshall and I have always had a good relationship in that respect because we can calmly talk about almost anything. This isn't the case with all family members and you have to be choosy about who you bring into the business based on that factor. You can't afford to try and make everyone happy or include everyone just to make peace. This is business, and you have to get the right person in the right place and pass on the individuals that will cause chaos.

From Dust to Diamonds
Empowering Your Team

I can't stress strongly enough the power of choosing the right people. As a start up entrepreneur, one of the hardest things to do is let go and trust the people you have hired to make the right decisions. But as the business grows this becomes necessary.

I've seen it numerous times where the entrepreneur becomes a bottleneck in his own company because he/she has to make the final decision on everything. But you eventually have to hand some of that power off if you are really going to grow.

I can tell you right now that I would take someone with good decision making skills over a Harvard educated newbie any day of the week because decision making is a learned skill that comes from experience. No one teaches it and you can't learn it by reading a book. It takes real world knowledge. That doesn't mean that your team of people isn't going to make mistakes on occasion, they will, but how you handle and react to those mistakes will determine the quality of team you end up with.

For example, if one of your team members tries something new and it doesn't work, you can't rant and rave at them or they will never take any sort of risk again. You must calmly sit with them and evaluate the results, see what there is to learn and encourage them to use that knowledge to choose better next time. You might think that it would be better for them not to take risk but again, that doesn't move you forward. Your team needs to learn what you know, and be able to make decisions that benefit the business as a whole. You can't be everywhere or make every decision because that would take all your time and slow things down tremendously.

As your business grows you need to free up your time to focus on the strategic running of the business, not make decisions on what kind of envelopes the office should use. I see this all the time, owners of multi-million dollar businesses can be so controlling that they insist on making every single decision while allowing their business to stagnate and then deteriorate. You must trust the people you hire and if you don't, fire them and get someone you can trust.

At one time, Oreck employed literally thousands of people across the country and it ran quite smoothly because I had good people in place and they had the authority to do their jobs well. But you can't think that you will get your company to that point in just a few years. It takes time and along the way there will inevitably be hiccups and hard times. Your staff will watch your demeanor and actions during these hard times and that will determine how hard they work for you.

A Little Gratitude Goes a Long Ways

There is a popular show of the day called Undercover Boss that allows a CEO to be disguised and work at the entry level jobs in their company for a week. For almost all of them it is an eye opening experience because very few ever worked those jobs or if they did, it has been decades. You can get so wrapped up in the daily pressures that you forget about all those people who are working hard to make your company a success. Showing appreciation and gratitude is extremely important and even more so if you are working with family. We tend to take people for granted yet without them we would have virtually nothing.

Yes, I worked very hard when it was just me with a vacuum under one arm doing my best impression of Willy Loman as I traveled around the country. Fast forward 40 years and the company is one of the most recognized brands in the country and I know it is not because I did it all myself. I had help, great help, for decades that allowed the company to grow tremendously. I am grateful to all those who helped make that happen and for any entrepreneur, gratitude and humility are important concepts because life has a way of humbling you when you don't take them to heart.

Oreck Wisdom:

Always look for way to improve the value
of your product to your consumer.

David Oreck

6

LEARN FROM EVERYONE

David Oreck

Chapter 6
Learn from Everyone

I get asked a lot where I learned all these business concepts – like there's some kind of course you can take. Well, actually, there is a course and its called life. You jump in there and do it. You have to be willing to learn and I don't mean just from so-called experts. You can learn from every situation, both good and bad. It might be learning more about your customers, your competitors, or even more about yourself but if you keep your mind open to ideas all the time then you have the opportunity to apply those lessons and figure out what works.

One of the reasons I'm writing my own experience down now is that maybe you can learn from some of that experience. I'm not saying I'm the most educated or absolute best business person on the planet, I'm not, but if you can take one little kernel of an idea from this book and apply it to your business then reading this has been worthwhile – and that's how I look at every single experience I have even today. If I can learn something then the time investment is well spent.

I will warn you that one thing that has no place in business is arrogance. In fact, if you want to be completely humbled just start to think you're the best thing since sliced bread. The market can and will bring you to your knees so don't ever think that you know it all or that you've arrived because that is nuts. Always be willing to accept new ideas and push yourself into the future.

Like I said, you can learn a little bit everywhere if you choose to and that has certainly been the case with me. I didn't learn much about marketing from General Sarnoff way back in the early days. I don't think that marketing was all that important during that time simply because his business existed in a time of short supply and high demand. This meant customers came to him, he didn't have to entice them. However, business strategy and how to handle adversity were things he really excelled at and I watched and learned. Sarnoff was a forward thinker and something you don't see much these days. Business to him was like a big chess match, he was always thinking three steps ahead of the other guy and that was a great lesson for me.

You can't just focus on today's bottom line – you have to think about where that bottom line will be a year from now or two years from now.

Sarnoff had a lot of confidence in what he believed even though it put his career at stake. Pursuing the RCA method of color television could have cost him his livelihood and his future. He literally bet the farm on his new technology and lost the first round because the FCC approved the CBS technology ahead of his. Unfortunately for CBS it wasn't a good choice and didn't work in the long run, but to believe that you could beat the government or a government agency where no one is accountable, now that takes a lot of smarts and an absolute belief in himself and his abilities. In the long run, Sarnoff was right and he prevailed. Witnessing that situation early in my career has helped me have the guts to carry on in my own business when things looked bleak or when other people said I was crazy to keep at it.

One case in point would be my long time accountant, who's now deceased, but I have a lot of love and respect for him. When I got in the vacuum business, I was also a wholesaler for RCA at the same time. That was making a profit. Whatever money I made, I lost on the vacuum cleaner business - or "invested" in the vacuum cleaner business I should say.

From Dust to Diamonds

My accountant told me on more than one occasion to get out of the vacuum cleaner thing and really that was probably good advice from where he stood because at the time it was draining my funds like a bad habit. But that was one time I didn't take his advice. I don't know if it is tenacity or guts or pure stupidity that tells you to continue when your best counselors tell you to get out but in the case of The Oreck Corporation I didn't listen. If I had it would have never prevailed and the company would never have become the success it could have been.

Now make no mistake, I've been in other businesses before that didn't work and I got out. I knew when to quit. For example, I had a little company that made grandfather clocks at one time and we were selling them, but I didn't account for one thing: I could sell them but not deliver them in one piece. The clock would bounce around in the truck and if there was even one little scratch, as is the case with furniture, the customer would refuse it. I could make them, I could sell them, but couldn't deliver them. So I had to ultimately get out of the business.

I've learned some things since that I would have done differently, but I got out of it because I didn't have a solution to that one problem. Not all businesses have all the pieces that fit together and sometimes you aren't at the place where you know enough to make that particular business work. It takes both.

I've always had some sort of side business – sometimes more than one – and I've learn a lot from them. While at RCA, I had a sort of scandal sheet newsprint television guide that I ran. But one of my boss's relatives owned the competing television guide at the time (in fact it would later become TV Guide) and so that didn't work and I saw that it was let it go or get fired. It was definitely a lesson in the politics of business.

At one time I had a small airplane charter business. That was a good business and at the time I thought I'd just about cornered the travel market in clandestine love affairs as that seemed to be the focus of many a passenger. I was also flying around Cardinal Spellman who was the head of the Catholic Church in New York so that was interesting. The charter business was a viable business but not one I could really devote enough time to.

**David Oreck 1955 with his
Ercoupe airplane**

I wasn't ready to take the leap away from my RCA job at that time so I got out of that one as well. The business was good, but the timing was bad. One other interesting business I had in New York was the forerunner of what would eventually become cable TV. We would put a very large antenna on the top of a building and would then run cables to each apartment. But again that job took lots of time, energy and service and the bottom line was, it was just a mess.

Some businesses I gave up more or less because I didn't want to stay and fight because it might put my main job at stake. I had to be very careful. I was doing a good job and we (RCA) were number one, and I was in the number one city in the country so my position couldn't have been better. I liked what I was doing with these side businesses, but I simply couldn't devote the time to them. I did all these with a very limited budget and I wasn't getting rich. I had a good paying job, supporting a wife and children. We lived moderately well, took vacations and sent the kids to private schools, but I didn't have a whole lot of wiggle room financially as most people didn't in those days.

About the time I turned 40, I finally felt it was time to leave my RCA job. I was running all sales at the RCA distributorship in New York by then. I just felt I'd had enough and wanted to do something on my own. When I left that job, I was doing nothing, so I was open to whatever opportunity came along. I didn't want to take a job with someone else because I had left that and didn't want to return to it. The vacuum thing came along, but honestly it could have been a widget of any kind. I worked under an exclusive agreement with Whirlpool to distribute their vacuums for the entire U.S. market.

As I shared earlier, once I dared to dip my toes in the area of direct mail, the president of Sears Roebuck, who was on the Whirlpool board, said, "Get rid of that guy", meaning me, and they (Whirlpool) did. That year I had purchased 100,000 vacuum cleaners from Whirlpool and they were really selling which was a phenomenal amount of product to move for one guy so I was upset with their decision to say the least.

Here again in business, sometimes the worst thing that can happen to you is the best thing that can happen to you because you are forced to get creative and take a road you might not have traveled. If they hadn't let me go, I would never have gone out on my own under my own name.

I had made my own bed and forced myself into this spot because I quit my job that I was doing very well at, in order to do something that no one knew about or cared about. I had to swing the whole thing myself and everything rested on my shoulders: financing, producing, marketing, advertising, and service. I really wasn't well equipped for all that, particularly the money part.

If someone came to me today with the same circumstances I was facing then and asked me if they should keep going, I'd ask if they were out of their mind – exactly the same reaction my accountant had all those years ago. I'd ask, 'How are you going to do this? Who's going to service it? How are you going to pay for it?' I know the answer and that is, it can be done but only if you are committed to being creative and doggedly persistent. I'd say that 99.9% of people just aren't that committed.

Tough situations create tremendous opportunity and you have to see that silver lining and keep moving forward if you ever expect to be successful. Small business can become big business but it doesn't just happen.

What makes a business successful is ideas, and ideas are everywhere. You can let yourself get so caught up in the daily slogging you just don't see them anymore.

The Creative Spark

I wasn't born particularly creative, but over the years, there were other people I learned from who were very creative. Gerald O. Kaye was the sales manager at one time in New York City at the RCA wholesale distributorship. He was a marketing man and I learned a lot about advertising from him. As a matter of fact, he tapped into some creative juices I didn't know I had. I got the hang of it pretty quickly. Gerald was very creative and knew his stuff as far as advertising goes. But the general manager, his boss (and mine) was the type that, the minute

Gerald would come in with a good ad, and before he even looked at the ad, he'd reach in his desk and pull out his pencil to correct it.

The general manager didn't know squat about advertising but he would try to correct Gerald, who was very good, very creative and knew his job. Eventually Gerald became frustrated and left. I succeeded him and I knew after watching Gerald that I'd never discount or criticize good ideas because they are very hard to come by.

I'm not saying the general manager was a bad guy – quite the opposite. He gave me an opening that was very good and I learned a great deal from him but I also learned that people frequently have specific skills. They are rarely good at everything. They may play the violin but can't tap dance. That doesn't make them a lousy violin player; it makes them a lousy tap dancer. This guy was a great manager, but didn't know anything about writing advertising copy and his ignorance cost him a great creative mind. The point is you can learn a lot from anyone if you just pick out what they're good at and let go of all the things they don't do well. You can never presume that because you are good at one thing, you're excellent at everything.

I've learned bits and pieces, and gotten some great ideas, often from unlikely sources and I will encourage you to always keep your eyes and ears open. I could occasionally walk back in the warehouse and hear something that sparked an idea if I had an open mind. You can go to a trade show to see what the trend is in colors and suddenly encounter someone who can help you in a completely different area.

You may see what someone else is doing that doesn't apply to your product at all but maybe some aspect of the way they are doing business or marketing their product does apply. What was once called plagiarism is now called 'research' and I would say I'm good at 'research'; seeing some little spark of an idea and translating it into something that can benefit my business. I'd readily admit that I'm not trying to reinvent the wheel. I want to learn as much as I can from someone else's experience so I don't have to make their mistakes all over again and so should you. I always tell entrepreneurs that you have two ears and one mouth, use them proportionately.

Really successful entrepreneurs must have an open mind and be willing to learn constantly. You can easily get to a point where you think you're so important that you're above learning or listening.

I tell people all the time to listen to their customers, but I'm still dumbfounded at how few actually do. A lot of people are great talkers but not good listeners and that will severely handicap their success. It is a critical thing – the ability to listen, learn and have an open mind. Of course, you've got to have some smarts too. You can't be a complete nitwit!

Part of being creative is having some degree of intuitiveness which is important. You have to have some sort of gut feel for when to take advice and when not to. So-called conventional wisdom generally isn't wise at all and you have to be able to be able to weed out the crap as you go. I will tell you that a lot of our modern education suppresses this intuitive instinct because it focuses so hard on teaching us 'rules': do this, don't do that. It doesn't invite the curious mind that believes there is a better way. You have to question, in the case of education, that if the teacher doesn't have that particular skill, how can he possibly teach the student?

I've spoken at more than 60 universities over the years and on one of those occasions, a professor asked me, "How do you teach intuitiveness?" I had to quiet the smart ass in me that wanted to say, "If you have to ask that, you don't have it!" Intuitiveness isn't something you teach, it is a natural instinct that has to be developed and over time most of our business training does just the opposite and suppresses it. The real question is, "How do you develop an intuitive mind?" In my case, it was a lot of trial and error. I have a good idea when something will work, but may not know exactly how. So I'll experiment and keep at it until I find the right combination of things that make it work.

I think sometimes business people get the mindset that if they try it once and it doesn't work, then it is a bad idea but that's rarely the case. Your intuition is probably right about the idea, but the execution takes time to develop.

How do you, while trying to stay focused, know when to seek a new idea and how to identify a good idea when it happens? When do you start? When do you stop? When do you know it is a lemon? It is a very difficult thing. If someone has a good idea, and then fails, people will say, well he was stubborn. If you have a good idea and persist, and it takes off, they say you're a genius. Hindsight makes it easy to see the diamonds and the dogs but it is not that easy up front.

I think that the biggest thing of all is to recognize and identify a problem that people have – a need. If you can recognize a need, you can solve it but if you can't see the issue, you're sunk.

Most great ideas are simple, like the light bulb. People had used fire, candles and lanterns for thousands of years, but one day a guy (Thomas Edison) realized that each of these light delivery methods was problematic. They needed messy and inconvenient fuel sources. They gave off too much heat or they didn't provide enough light exactly where it was needed. The story goes that he made up to 10,000 prototypes of the light bulb before he got one that functioned and worked well. He had a great, simple creative idea: deliver cheap, safe, convenient indoor lighting. He knew it was a great idea intuitively and then demonstrated the creativity and persistence necessary to make it work.

You don't have to create a new light bulb (although that would be a great idea), and it is true that my vacuums aren't on the level of that great creation but they solved a basic problem that people have every day. They want clean carpets! Simple, but I had to stick with the idea until I developed a creative solution to their problem that was unique and different.

David Oreck

Oreck Wisdom:

Not only is it imperative to identify
the customer, you must identify
the customer who can purchase today!

David Oreck

THE LOST ART OF MARKETING

David Oreck

Chapter 7
The Lost Art of Marketing

Experience is the best teacher in the world and the only way to get that experience is to try different approaches and see what works. The good news is that you can learn anything if you want to; the bad news is that most people dip a toe in the water and instead of wading in, they want to do a cannon ball off the highest cliff – such as it is with marketing. No one has an unlimited budget and for those just starting out, it is crucial that what budget you do have is spent on getting you customers, not guessing. It is not about putting all your money on a red number nine and rolling the dice.

I test every marketing strategy, and then I review that data to see what seems to be resonating with consumers. This isn't about quantifying results or sales figures; it is about seeing what is getting people to take action and respond. Once they respond, then we have the opportunity to sell them. That is just as true today as it was 40 years ago. The ads and media outlets may have changed, but consumers haven't so if you allow them to tell you how they want to buy, and then listen, you can be successful. You may think that's easy for me to say that because my company is successful, but I continue to learn even now.

It doesn't matter if you buy an existing business or if you start one from scratch with a great new product, the process is essentially the same. Of course, knowing what I know now if I were going to choose a business I'd buy one that had at least some brand recognition even if it was lying dormant or fallow. That is how important I feel brand recognition is, not just because it gives you a marketing advantage, but more because I know how hard it is to build any type of recognition. It takes time and money, and then often years to come to fruition.

Of course, if you have a new idea that solves a basic problem then you certainly can pursue it, but just realize that the research and development costs are going to add up and it is important to prepare yourself. For example, I saw a great new product on CNN called Idea Paint. It is basically paint that turns any wall into a dry erase board. Great idea! The story chronicled the quest of the entrepreneurs and how they tried and failed and tried and failed again with formula after formula.

When they finally got one that worked, they were nearly bankrupt but with a product to show were able to get financing to produce and market it. They kept trying because they knew they had an idea that would revolutionize the 30 million dollar dry erase market.

It is wonderful to have a great idea but remember that the costs to develop something new can be substantial, even if it is a new or uniquely designed product that people already recognize, like a new vacuum. You have manufacturing costs that really drain the budget well in advance of even trying to sell the thing so you can't afford to make a lot of mistakes with your money when it comes time to market. You can't necessarily do a fully fledged marketing campaign and why would you want to at this stage? You don't even really know for certain who your customers are so why would you do a big campaign on a guess? You may think you know who they are, but do you really?

If you've been in business for any length of time at all, you have probably been humbled by customers a time or two. I don't mean they put you in your place, but just that they didn't act, respond or behave the way you predicted so you were stuck with a lot of product and not much in sales. This has happen to me more than a few times over the years and taught me that no matter what my assumptions are, it is important to test the market and confirm what I think to be true before I dump a truckload of money into any one type of marketing.

I learned a long time ago that one of the best avenues to create great brand recognition, ongoing sales and customer loyalty is to deal with the customer direct. This gives the opportunity to educate the consumer without a lot of competition. As you build on that customer relationship you continue to create value by standing behind your product and offering the kind of service that creates long term loyalty. The beauty of this avenue of marketing is that it allows the small entrepreneur or one person type organization the ability to test their message and then refine it as they learn more about the customers who buy and how to reach them more effectively.

Once again, being small is a real advantage. The small business has to focus and produce results quickly whereas a large corporation can throw lots of money into marketing but may not be nearly as effective in terms of return on that effort.

Step-by-Step Marketing

If you want to define your customers either because you are just starting out and don't know who they are, or if you are introducing a new product and expanding your customer base, there are several small steps you can take.

First and foremost you have to define your message. You have to choose two or three features of your product or service that are unique and different even if your product is similar to others on the market. It has to have something unique otherwise you have nothing to offer. In my case, it was the fact that my vacuum was only eight pounds. So lightweight was one of the key features my marketing focused on. Another one was that it could stand up to commercial use. So the idea that hotel maids used my product was a key idea. You can't have a laundry list because it is confusing and you lose the audience. Pick one or two.

A good example is Geico Insurance. To most consumers car insurance is car insurance and everyone wants to save a buck, but Geico realized one of the customers' biggest frustrations was that it was hard to get a quote quickly and find good, inexpensive insurance. So rather than focusing on all the different types of insurance they offered they focused on two ideas: fast quotes and saving money. They use the line in every ad, "15 minutes can save you 15% or more on car insurance."

This is very effective because it focuses on something different that consumers weren't getting from the other guys. I have no idea if they have great insurance, but I can tell you they have great marketing. While they are the fourth largest auto insurer in the U.S., they are number one in attracting new customers as reported in an article by Advertising Age. Now make no mistake they are playing on a national field, but it is an illustration of the fact that even the little guy can be an all-star if he figures out how to give customers what they really want.

Once you have identified the few ideas you want to highlight for your product, you have to develop ad copy. You want to try a couple of different angles so play with the ideas and think of ads that have appealed to you in the past. Probably most of them will include some type of humor because humor is memorable and unique – and hard to get right if you are writing it, so work on it until you get something that really speaks to people.

You can also use illustration or demonstration. We have used the hotel maid holding our vacuum over her head for years as it immediately conveys lightweight and heavy duty performance.

I developed the idea of showing how the little four pound vacuum cleaner that we offered with our regular unit could lift a 16 pound bowling ball. The suction on this little thing was really strong and I thought that showing it could lift something four times its own weight with that suction was a real winner as far as a visual was concerned. So the plan was that I was going to make the commercial, but I was on a trip during these discussions and so my brother, Marshall, coordinated the shoot.

"Some people stand behind their products, I stand under mine."

Take the Oreck Challenge. Try to find products that are backed by stronger warranties than mine. For example, the Super Celoc 2-motor Canister/ Upright has a full 7-year warranty. The housing on my 8-pound Oreck XL is not one or two years, it's ten years.

And as you've seen in my national TV commercials my products, made right here in America, are so incredibly powerful that I also stand under them. And I challenge you to find anyone else who does.

Be sure to take advantage of my new Oreck Power Card. It's your direct credit line to my best products and gives you tremendous savings. With the Oreck Power Card, there are no finance charges, no interest payments. (See other side for details.) Nobody makes it easier for you to own great home-care products than I do.

You can be confident of getting assistance from our staff, 24 hours a day, 7 days a week. A network of over 600 service centers are available throughout the U.S. With all Oreck products, remember, if you don't love them, just send them back.

ORECK
Nothing gets by an Oreck.

Ad showing the incredible power of our small canister vacuum.

The producer of the commercial told my brother, "We will hold the small vacuum, and show that it is lifting the bowling ball. Then we will prove how strong it is by having it hold the bowling ball over your brother's head." Now this is a 16 pound bowling ball – so no small matter.

My brother pointed out, "Well you know, you better be careful with that because if you had a power failure, that 16 pound bowling ball would drop right on his head."

The producer didn't even bat an eye and said, "Well, we'll make that the last scene we build." So they did and thankfully my head survived just fine!

The idea was to convey just how well our product worked and consumers responded. That kind of visual is hard to beat and you see this sort of demonstration used all the time in commercials and infomercials. Show the consumer the problem and then show them that you have the solution.

The next step is to test the message. No matter the advertising medium, you have the option to test various ideas on various types of customers and you can choose who gets what. For example, if you are doing television you can choose channels that are produced for particular demographic groups. For example, if you want to focus on educated adults that are relatively affluent you would be able to choose various educational and cultural channels whose audience is that target market. The same is true with print, radio and direct mail. Those media outlets will be able to help you drill down the specifics you want to target as they all keep very specific records on which demographics they serve. You don't have to guess or make assumptions when they have actual data to use.

If you are just starting out, it is okay to start small even if the media representative tries their hardest to sell you a bigger marketing package. They are paid on commission so of course they want you to buy more, but that will come later. At first you want to be sure it is working so it is okay to start small and test it out. If one ad works better than another, then that is great information you can then use to make the dollars you spend tomorrow more effective than the ones you spent yesterday.

When I test an ad, I always use some identifier so I know what business came from which ad. For example, I'll include a special code they input, or if its mail response I'll include a specific department number like Dept. 10 or Dept. 11. That way I can tell if it came from a mail drop in a certain neighborhood or part of the country and when it was done. You see this all the time – even on television they will have you call a specific number or give a 'special' code to get a gift and that is all so the advertiser can determine who is buying and what advertising is motivating them to buy. This way, the data you collect is much more specific.

One of the ways I tested my ads were to try one that included a price and then one that didn't. What I found was that there was a much higher response from the ad that didn't have a price. People would request information or call in and ask the price. This gave us the opportunity to convert them to a sale right there, or at least educate them on the value they are receiving.

One of the drawbacks of advertising is that space is limited so you need to find a way to get them to contact you. Even if they don't buy at first, you have gotten their information and can add them to your regular contact list to receive ongoing offers or catalogs.

Over time, as you are defining your customer, you are gathering data and compiling your customer contact base. This base will someday be the backbone of your business and a very valuable way to market more or new products to your customers. You may think that all of this is a lot of work when you can simply run an ad anywhere and see how it flies, and it is some work to be sure. But it can really benefit you in the long run in several ways.

First of all you know exactly who and where your customers are and how to get to them. This saves time, energy and money in every way. You can think of it like this: suppose you are trying to find all the white mice in an old mansion.

There are gray mice, field mice, spiders, bats and all sorts of other creatures you don't want, but you need to find the white mice. Now you can spend lots of money laying hundreds of mouse traps all over the place because you have no idea where this type of mouse is or what it likes to eat – or you can test several locations and several types of bait first.

You might set 20 traps just in the kitchen with cheddar cheese (one kind of message), and then set 20 traps in the living room with peanut butter (another type of message). These are two specific locations with two different messages so you have to give that time to work and check the results.

Let's say you wait a week and check your traps. In the kitchen you have 14 empty traps and six traps with mice but no white mice. Hmm – very few mice and none of your target variety so obviously that message isn't being very effective and the location may have issues too. Next, you check the living room and you have 16 traps with mice and 12 white mice – a great result. This message and location might have real promise.

Now you have to determine if it is the location or the message, so you switch the bait (message) and try those same two areas again.

This time in the kitchen you have 16 empty traps, but you have caught four white mice with the peanut butter. In the living room, you have 11 full traps and four of them are white mice.

From this little scenario I would conclude two things: first there are more white mice in the living room than the kitchen that will respond to my messages. Second, my target mice (white mice) love peanut butter. Now I know that if I focus my efforts on the living room and stick to the peanut butter message, I will get a lot more white mice with less money spent and less effort.

While the scatter gun approach of setting traps all over the place might get you a few mice of some sort, the information you gain is useless because you have no idea where they came from or what message was effective. You are not spending your money wisely or efficiently because you are just hoping to catch the right mice.

From Dust to Diamonds

Hunting customers is the same way. Sure you can blast indiscriminate advertising out there but you'll spend a lot of money and time and have mediocre results at best. Better to test and see what message gets the most response from your target market first.

Another way that this data can really serve you is if you find yourself in need of financing. Whether you go to a bank for a loan, or approach an individual to invest, you have to show them something to help them see that you know what you are doing and that your idea has promise. Hard data helps that cause tremendously.

Let's say an entrepreneur sits down in front of a banker or potential investor and says "I have this new product and I'm convinced that it will be the next big thing but I need some money to get it to market." This entrepreneur may have the prettiest financials, pro forma and cash flow spreadsheets but so does everyone else they have seen that day. When the investor asks, "Who is the customer and how are you going to market to them?" The entrepreneur better have something to offer. If he/she says that their market is 'everyone' and they plan to buy radio and television ads, would you give him/her money? Probably not.

On the other hand, if the entrepreneur says, "I've test marketed several ads in two different media – television and direct mail. My data shows my customer is a 35-60 year old female in a two income household, well educated with disposable income. The print ad had a response rate of 2% and a conversion rate of 30% of those that responded. The television ad had a response rate of 1% and a conversion rate of 25% of those that responded. I plan to market my product using a 70/30 mix of both these media outlets focusing on print ads." Now would you give him money? Probably so, because he has done his homework and knows his target customer so he's way ahead of what most investors see from business people on a daily basis.

Knowing exactly who the customer is and how to reach them is imperative to every aspect of your business from marketing to new product design, and gives you great data to build your business on.

David Oreck
The Message

One of the most frequent questions I get is, "How do I figure out my message?" I can't tell you exactly because I don't know your product, but I can give you some examples and show you how to figure it out.

A few years ago I was speaking at a college and afterward I asked the students for questions. One guy stood up and said that he had a pool cleaning business in the summer and he wanted to expand his business.

The first goal was to find what was unique about his business. I'd be the first to say I don't know a hell of a lot about pool cleaning but I have owned a pool before so I know that every pool cleaner says they clean pools. So what is your message? That you clean them better? No. Everyone says that too, so it is meaningless and just puts you right in the running with the competition.

Now having owned a pool, I can tell you a big issue is a slippery deck so I suggested that this guy might start advertising that he specializes in deck treatment which gives homeowners a safer pool with no mildewed deck in addition to a clean pool. He thought it was a great idea. That's what I mean about looking for one great feature or benefit. You can't choose the ones that are the same as everyone else. You have to be different.

A good exercise is to gather up a bunch of ads from your competition and see what benefits of their products they are promoting – then don't do that! It seems pretty obvious that you should do something different, but you would be shocked at how many people just do copycat advertising.

If a big company starts one kind of ad, then the next thing you know there are lots of copycats – even if the ad isn't all that effective. The little guy has to dare to be different and unique or he'll never stand out the way he has to.

The message you present is key and will be something that you massage and tweak all the years you are in business so it bears a lot of attention and scrutiny. Every message can be better or can speak to a different segment of the market. The idea isn't to get the perfect message and use it forever, but to find the message that gets you the target audience you are after for that particular product and puts money in your pocket instead of a hole.

Managing Expectations

Everyone goes into business with the best case scenario in mind. Of course we do; if we didn't think we'd be successful we'd never start. But many entrepreneurs set completely unrealistic goals for themselves and this can have a devastating effect on their state of mind and eventually their business. I've seen it many times when someone says, "Well in the first quarter our goal is 5% of the total market share and then by the end of next year we anticipate we'll have 10%." Even if you have the best product that people have seen in ten years, it takes time to market, manage and then grow that business. It doesn't happen in a year or even two or three in most cases.

It is important to understand all the forces at work so you can manage your own expectations. By this I mean understanding that a 5% market share in one year is huge for most new products and that sustaining growth of even a few percentage points per year equates to explosive growth. Setting a goal that is completely off the charts gives the entrepreneur a panicked feeling of urgency that does not necessarily lead to the best business decisions. For example, if a business person expects to double or triple the size of his business in order to hit his projected market share he might not take the time to test his marketing and end up with very disappointing results.

By focusing on something that is way ahead of where you are, you might also start making choices that will actually kill growth rather than encourage it.

I've seen many entrepreneurs rent big offices or big warehouses with the idea they would 'grow' into them, but when their growth doesn't happen as quickly as they thought it would they are stuck with huge overhead that eats into their budget for marketing and everything else.

As a small business person it is much better to pick a small segment in maybe one neighborhood, one town or one region. Start small and learn those lessons early. Don't be afraid to look small – it is better to be a big fish in a small pond than a guppy in the ocean so keep that in mind. You don't have to put up a false front of being big and impressive. If you have a good product no one cares if you have an expensive office. As I said earlier, for years we shipped product out of a semi trailer we had parked not too far from my brother's home. That worked for us for quite a while. We didn't need a big warehouse yet because we weren't to that point as far as our sales were concerned.

Today's business environment offers a lot of opportunity for people to work from home and I'd suggest to any entrepreneur to stay in the basement as long as they can. By that I mean keep your overhead low, work at your marketing and learn to dominate a small segment of the market before you try to take on the world.

It is not that we don't dream of being the big dog someday – we all do. But you just have to allow yourself time to grow and learn the lessons along the way that will keep you in business and build your company for years to come.

Oreck Wisdom:

This is the age of marketing... the trick is in the selling, not the making.

David Oreck

THE BULLDOG MENTALITY

David Oreck

Chapter 8
The Bulldog Mentality

The mental side of being a business owner is much harder than the physical obstacles that you encounter on a daily basis. The ability to keep your head straight and not panic when things hit the fan is critical in making good decisions. Of course we're all human and there are going to be times that circumstances really get you down, but the bulldog mentality can be learned and experience can be your best teacher. The issues I encountered early on with my vacuum business helped me gain that type of mentality and as time went on, things bothered me less and less. Part of this is because early on, it was hard to see how things would work out but as I tried various approaches and worked through the problems, I gained more confidence that I could take on anything that came my way. Of course now hindsight is 20/20 and it is clear what the solutions were but at the time it was not clear at all and I often felt as if I was walking a very shaky wire thousands of feet above the ground.

At several points I thought the business was completely in the dumpster. When I was initially forced to stop manufacturing under the Whirlpool brand I was counting on and switch the company name to Oreck, I could have quit. It would have been much easier – and definitely cheaper.

But I wanted to prove that it would work and that I could overcome anything they threw my way. The company expenses bled my own personal funds on a regular basis and even when my accountant said I should quit, I refused.

Entrepreneurs have to cultivate their belief in themselves. There are thousands of people who will gladly tell you how wrong you are, why you should give up and why you were crazy to ever think of being in business in the first place. There are very few who will encourage you or show you the way. You have to accept that fact and when someone does offer advice (from experience in their own business) you should listen and then only take from them what you can use and apply. Throughout this book I've offered a lot of advice, every bit of it based on my last 70 years in business. There may be some things you can use and some that you can't - the task for you is to take what you can and apply it and even if you get one idea that makes your business better or more successful then this has been worth it.

The Devil You Know

There are many ways to start a business. These include your own money, investors, loans and a few other avenues like venture capitalists. There are many needs for capital in a business whether it be growth, capital investment or miscellaneous expenses. I see entrepreneurs seek financing in a variety of ways and none of them is really wrong, you just want to be sure who you are getting in bed with. It is a trite cliché to say look before you leap, especially if someone is waving a check under your nose, but there are important considerations that come along with any type of outside financing and it can have tremendous ramifications on the direction of your business either from a positive or negative standpoint.

I used my own money to start my business and over the years used loans on occasion to satisfy capital needs. I never really wanted to take on partners and liked the fact I had the last word and didn't have to worry about some board of directors or partner that might not agree with what I wanted to accomplish. When I wanted to exit the business I sold it to some venture capitalists and this is the path that many entrepreneurs think about traveling.

Build it from nothing, sell it for a profit and go your merry way. But it is not as easy as that so I'd like to insert a little cautionary note for your consideration.

No matter who gives you money, there are always strings attached even if they say there aren't. There are; bet on it. Investors want to see a return and bankers want you to be able to pay your note. That's fine, you say, you knew that going in. But what about when they start insisting that you do less marketing or that you pursue one market over another or just generally start messing in your business? They have money at stake too, so they will interfere at some point and it may be more or less severe but it will happen. It is another layer of irritation and stress you don't need so you better be sure you are prepared for it.

As is the case with overambitious sales figures, an entrepreneur can really get themselves in a fix if they rely on those ambitious numbers to secure financing. Then they have to deal with reality, but reality isn't what you sold the investors or the bank on. What now?

How easy will it be for you to keep your determined attitude when you are getting questioned from all sides? It is hard enough to make good decisions when it is just you in your head, but when you add a banker or investors that want results it gets pretty crowded. This is a situation where testing your marketing and conversion rates will keep you out of trouble. Good numbers don't lie and while you may like to fool yourself and think you'll have a 25% market share in a year, the numbers will tell you otherwise and those are numbers you can really believe.

The main reason I'm not a big fan of taking on partners or sharing decision making as an entrepreneur is that group think rarely provides the best outcome. It turns into a contest between risk and security. The entrepreneur knows that he must takes risks to get anywhere, but the partner or banker may want to protect the asset and so it sets up a natural battle line. The odds of you having a great business relationship are pretty long and about the same as having a long and happy marriage. It can happen, but it doesn't happen often. When money is involved people get emotional very quickly and those emotions may be directed right at the entrepreneur.

Venture capitalists are in a little different category. I sold Oreck vacuums to a venture capitalist group because I was ready to retire and get some of my estate concerns taken care of.

My children didn't want the business and I was good with that; they each have their own successful lives. So the choice was beneficial for me. I agreed to stay around as spokesperson for commercials when they needed me, but that was it. They run the company.

What most people don't realize is that venture capitalists aren't your normal investors. They have a final goal in mind and that is to make the company as attractive as possible to another buyer or to take it public and cash out. Either way, they are in business to make as much profit as possible by buying and selling and the commodity they use is companies.

The problem for many entrepreneurs is that the goal sounds similar to what the business person has in mind, but it really isn't. The entrepreneur usually wants what they built to prosper as an entity, but it might end up a division of another company or with another name or as some other incarnation.

This can set up a real conflict if the entrepreneur is still involved in the business because now you have other people effectively running the business so employees may be treated differently, plant facilities may be moved, and marketing plans may be completely altered – and there isn't much you can do about it. That is why you will often see a company purchased by venture capitalists and the agreement includes a three or five year contract with the entrepreneur to stay on as CEO, but after a short time the entrepreneur and venture capitalists part ways because one entity needs to have the final say.

From Dust to Diamonds

It is like raising a child from birth and then someone takes over and does it differently. I'm not saying it's better or worse; it is just different, especially if the people taking over have different ultimate goals than you do. I'm not discouraging you from going down this path in any way, I just want you to investigate all the ramifications and be sure you can live with them before your jump in.

The vast majority of entrepreneurs do as I did and try to fund their companies mostly on their own and while this is a struggle in the beginning, it gives you ultimate control and direction over the business which can reduce the type of stress you encounter by constantly explaining every decision to others who don't really understand what you are trying to accomplish.

There is nothing wrong with partners, investors or anyone who wants to be a part of growing your business, just be very aware of the need for additional communication and possible pitfalls - especially when money is involved. I've seen many a business abandoned just over money squabbles that weren't all that big a deal, but the investors or partners couldn't work it out and chose to give up instead. Be cautious and guard your business and your dream.

The Myth of the Economy

One of the hardest ideas to grasp mentally is the power that small businesses have. According to the Small Business Administration, there are in excess of 27 million small businesses (defined as those with less than 100 employees).

Now to some of you, 100 employees sounds small but the reality is that 99.9 percent of small businesses have less than four employees. Four. So why would you sit in your home office feeling small?

Every day on the news, we see thousands of people being laid off and huge corporations going under or being exposed in some new scandal. It seems like business is crumbling all around us and it can be easy to think that now is not a good time to start your own operation or grow an existing business. But think about this. Those reports concern a very tiny portion of businesses in the US. They aren't talking about the millions of mom and pops across the country quietly growing their enterprises and flourishing.

It is like when you go to Las Vegas and see all the glittering resorts – those weren't built by whales or by the lucky few who win millions every trip. They were built by the little guys who gladly contributed their hard earned dollars on vacation for some fun and entertainment. Our country doesn't run on the giant corporations with 30,000 employees either. It runs via the contributions of all the small business entities that work day in, day out, growing their businesses, paying their taxes and employing millions of people.

For example, I just saw some numbers put out by the National Restaurant Association. They state that more than nine in ten restaurants (93%) are small businesses with less than 50 employees yet they are the nation's second largest private sector employer and job creator.

They currently employ more than 13 million people – almost ten percent of the current workforce. Every million dollars in restaurant sales generates 34 more jobs for the economy and that is a valuable contribution. You may feel small, grinding away in your little restaurant in Schenectady, but you are driving our economy to prosperity with your efforts.

I want to encourage you not to get caught in the trap of feeling like the smallest dog in the pack. Small can be great especially if you understand your customers in a way that big business never seems to. Entrepreneurs can create their own economy so it doesn't ever matter what the broader economy is, or isn't, doing; you will always be able to find a business or widget that is your golden goose.

Think back to where all the money came from to create the country we now live in. There weren't big corporations and multinational entities that employed millions two hundred years ago. But there were thousands and thousands of little guys who came here from all over the world to have a chance at owning their own business. These people took their little mercantile, transport, and service businesses and grew them – that is what built a nation and it is still occurring.

Every business has a life cycle. It starts small, grows in spurts over time and then becomes a large business until new products, services or technology replaces it and the cycle starts again. Expect that from your efforts as well. You can be the next Fortune 100 Company, but it is not going to happen in five years and it is not going to happen if you don't hang on with that bulldog mindset and keep plugging away until you find what works.

Vote with Your Cash

Anyone who has been around me for more than a few minutes knows that I'm a big proponent of buying American. This is more than just a patriotic notion – although I am very patriotic. We each have the opportunity as individuals and as business owners to contribute to our own economic salvation. Look back to that statistic I just listed that for every million dollars spent at restaurants, it produces 34 jobs. When I eat out at a local restaurant in New Orleans I think about that. I'm helping to improve the business of a local entrepreneur just like me and I'm helping to employ people who need the work.

I'm contributing to the welfare of the business, their employees, their suppliers and the families of all those people who depend on that stream of income. Literally thousands of people benefit from supporting just one local business. That is a great feeling.

Once you become an entrepreneur you realize how vital it is to 'vote with cash'. By this I mean that instead of getting frustrated with government policy and politicians who can't seem to find their butt with both hands, we each do what we can to support each other. That means buying your supplies from, and frequenting, local businesses.

Years ago this is what we did because the option of buying something from China, or anywhere else, just wasn't viable.

Over the last few decades as products have flooded in from other countries, many people have gravitated to them because of the low price. Large corporations also outsourced many functions such as call centers and manufacturing to parts of the world where labor is cheap. In my view this damaged our economy and over the last few years we're finally starting to see a backlash as more and more of the inferior products are determined to have damaging substances such as lead in them or are serving to chase customers away rather than retain them.

For example, when is the last time you called for computer support or to ask a question about your credit card statement and got a person who's first language was English? In fact there's a funny commercial out now that illustrates this point. A person calls on their credit card and gets a guy in Russia who says his name is Peggy. This illustrates how irritated customers are with these practices. Low price isn't always the best deal and it causes much more harm than good to our small businesses and overall economy.

This environment is also what I believe has shifted entrepreneurs from marketing the value of their products to customers because they think that it is all about price. Clearly it is not, or you could never sell a pair of blue jeans for $130. People around the world want good value and are willing to pay for it, so the assumption that price is the only key factor is wrong. Yet it is easy to understand why a new business person would assume it is because that's all they see – advertising that focuses on price.

Most people don't intend to harm their own economy, but it is easy not to pay attention when you are shopping and thus do so inadvertently. When was the last time you turned over a decorative item in a store to see where it was made? We cheat ourselves by buying cheap overseas merchandise as it pulls money out of our pocket to create jobs somewhere other than America. All I'm asking is that you let your cash do the talking and pay attention to purchasing those items made in America any time you have the opportunity.

I also encourage everyone to support your local small business people as an individual. They are your neighbors, friends and fellow Americans who are working hard to create their own mark in the world.

From Dust to Diamonds

It takes courage and hard work to step out on your own and they deserve your patronage just as you will deserve theirs when you are marketing your own product or services. By paying attention, we all benefit from a healthier, more robust economy that is putting more and more of us to work.

Oreck Wisdom:

There is only one boss in your business
-you want it to be you.

REAL GROWTH

David Oreck

Chapter 9
Real Growth

Once a business gets on its feet and starts to make a little money, the entrepreneur has to ask him/herself, now what? How do I grow this business? Growth is an interesting business concept because it is one of those areas where no matter who you ask, you will get a different answer. Many business experts will say expand, expand, expand – and while it is true that to grow you must expand some area of what you are doing, it is also a simplistic response to a very complex undertaking. It can be easy to think that growth means getting your product everywhere but here again, you have to go back to the fact that you must control your distribution. If you let loose of that distribution in the name of growth, then that distribution will eventually control you and instead of growing, you find yourself working harder and profiting less.

The necessity for growth is a given, but how that growth takes place will determine if your business eventually succeeds or fails – and yes there are many instances where a company or brand decided to grow, but they went about it in a way that ruined them. More isn't necessarily better; it is just more.

For example, one way that Oreck expanded was to open small local dealer stores that were exclusive distributors for that area – and many of these stores still exist. Those were very successful and many businesses expand by opening local stores in various areas. Now when your business grows, it is easy for the bean counters to look at the spreadsheets and think, "Well, if we can earn a little more by opening more stores we should do it." Not necessarily.

It is cheaper and easier to have individual stores each maximize their profit than to open new stores that may only be marginally successful. This was a conflict I faced as Oreck grew. Some of the management team was convinced that more stores meant more sales and that's all they saw. They didn't see near as much value in maximizing the existing distributors and offering them more support to make those stores as profitable as possible – and that's not the only issue.

When you have physical stores you increase overhead with each opening and have to start the local marketing from square one instead of building upon what you already have.

This is expensive and is still no guarantee of success because as you add stores, you are increasing overhead and risk while only hoping for a marginal gain. When you have a considered purchase, people will find it. You don't need more stores, you need more customers. But executives assume all the time that more stores means more profit and that is not always correct; so don't think that it is just the little guys that make these kinds of faulty assumptions. Almost every day it seems we are seeing large chains and retailers go under. Take the recent implosion of the Borders book store chain. For years they were all about expand, expand, expand. They built more than 1200 stores all over the place and tried to conquer the market by saturating areas with their retail outlets and it seemed they were successful soaring to the #1 book retailer in the early to mid 1990's.

But then in the late 1990's, the book business started to change. Amazon rose to first compete with the brick and mortar stores, but then soon dominated online book sales as consumer behavior shifted to buying online. Then the digital revolution hit and competitors such as Amazon and Barnes and Noble embraced e-books, developing their own e-readers to capitalize. Borders didn't. This illustrates one of the biggest risks business can face, and that's when your customers' behavior starts to shift.

Now the customer hasn't changed, but the way they buy books has and though it occurs over time sometimes that change is faster than you think. Now if you have long term leases on physical stores for the next 10 or 20 years and your profit falls every quarter, you can see the problem. Sales plummet, but all that overhead remains constant or rises each year, and the end is inevitable.

These issues all come back to the same problem: you must stay in touch with who your customer is and what they want. Borders forgot this and lost touch with their customers. They based decisions on customer behavior from the 1980's and didn't shift their strategy when that behavior changed. They went down so fast they couldn't even get a buyer interested! Who would have guessed in 2003, when they were flying high with 1200 stores worldwide that a mere eight years later they would be facing complete liquidation?

It is the height of arrogance for any business to have the attitude that the consumer will do what they dictate and will buy their product no matter what. It just isn't true. That kind of arrogance has taken down some of the biggest names in retail such as Sears, K-mart, and Woolworth's. I see this happening now with Wal-Mart and mark my words, they are in for a struggle in the coming years.

Don't ever forget your customer and don't load yourself up with so much overhead that you can't shift your focus when their behavior changes.

That's great for the big guys, you may think, but what about the little single person business that just has one product? How do I get it into retailers? Stop right there and think about what you are asking. One of the things that I have seen repeatedly is for inventors or product manufacturers to try and get their product into these large discount or big box stores like Best Buy. I'll admit on the surface, it sounds reasonable to the uninitiated that if you have a product you should try to get it in as many stores as possible, right? Wrong. We discussed this in an earlier chapter that if you have a considered purchase you must control your distribution or the distribution will control you. So it only makes sense to go to these retailers when you have the leverage of a solid brand just as in the example of Martha Stewart and Macy's.

A considered purchase is a brand named item that costs more, offers more value and gives the market something unique. I'm not talking about a pair of $10 sneakers – that is exactly the kind of product that Wal-Mart loves and if that is what you are producing then perhaps that is the best destination for you. What I am talking about is something like a high-end vacuum or other specialty product. I've repeatedly driven home the idea that not everyone is your customer. So why would you want to have your product in a store that serves the masses? You go from being unique and special to an 'also ran' offered in a discount store competing on price alone and as we've also discussed, price isn't the biggest part of the equation, value is. How can you possibly educate a customer about value if your product is just sitting on a shelf?

Low cost retailers are not your friend when you are trying to grow your business. They give you the illusion of growth on paper, while in reality they are killing your business. Like I said before, you are known by the company you keep which is why you don't see Tiffany's jewels at Wal-Mart. If the retailer stands for cheap and cut rate, then that image will rub off on your products. If the retailer stands for high end and exclusive, then that adds value to your product and brand.

The answer of course is to maintain very close control on your distribution. By doing so, you don't have a big retailer beating you up all the time to offer a cheaper version of your product or telling you what you will and will not develop. They also don't set unreasonable payment terms that could force your business to fold purely because of cash flow issues.

Once you get into a relationship with one or more of these big guys, you have lost control of your product and your brand and are at their mercy. Your profit margin will do nothing but decline to the point you can no longer stay in business at which time they will replace your product with a cheaper one from China or somewhere else in the world.

I've seen it happen over and over. And what about getting them to pay? Your very life is determined by when they finally decide to cut you a check for product you produced perhaps six or nine months earlier which is hard enough. But what if they decide to delay that payment? What then? Well unless you have a pile of cash buried in the backyard, you are done, and that is what you are agreeing to when you get into bed with a big discounter.

You also have to know that once you hand over your distribution, your brand name gets diluted to the point of being almost meaningless.

Here again that is because there is no one to educate the consumer on what your brand stands for or the kind of quality you deliver. So how can they really make any sort of informed decision based on anything but price?

I have been, and will always be, a big proponent of selling your product or service directly to the consumer. There is no need to involve a middle man at all and there is definitely more downside than up with big retailers. By selling direct you have 100% say over what you produce, how its produced, what features are, or are not, offered and how you get paid. No one else has the power to run you out of business. This is always the best case scenario and to my way of thinking, giving away control of any aspect of your business should never be considered.

Identity Crisis

As a company grows it is very important for the owners and managers to understand the company's brand and what they stand for as a company. There is nothing more confusing to a consumer than a company sending mixed messages about who they are. For example, let's think about Sears. When was the last time you were even in a Sears store? It has probably been a while if you even darken the door at all. Over the past two decades, Sears has been in a tailspin. This is largely because they have had an identity crisis and you can see this from some of their marketing. Sears was the Craftsman tool exclusive distributor –

and they built a huge following from the value of that brand. They also had great quality appliances with salespeople to help you and this was a big part of who they were.

Then mostly in the late 1980's and 1990's, they wanted to compete more in the clothing and home décor areas so we saw media campaigns about "Come see the softer side of Sears." They were mostly a flop as the clothing was marginal quality and people didn't really see Sears as that type of retailer. It is a big leap to go from being known as a tool and appliance retailer to a clothing store.

Over the last decade they have also handed over some distribution of their strong Craftsman brand. Now you can buy them at K-mart (owned by Sears), Ace Hardware, Amazon, EBay and a few other outlets.

Why would any of the hardcore Craftsman customers go to Sears now? I'm sure someone in an office somewhere thought that making that brand more available would make them more money. But all it did was decrease the foot traffic to their stores which has cost them big. Here again, they didn't understand the core principle that your customer is not everyone so why sell your product at a store that serves the masses? They were once able to attract a specific customer looking for a specific product and a specific brand but they let it go.

Sears has often been slammed by Wall Street for not investing to upgrade its stores and attract more customers, but I think the real problem is that they have lost sight of who their customer even is, and what will motivate them to buy today. They have a schizophrenic approach to their marketing if they even do any, which they haven't been much lately. They have added another 437 stores since 2006, yet their net sales have fallen $10 billion - and that is significant! In 2011 they named another CEO and he stated that they will be refocusing their efforts on building their home services and apparel lines. What?

Sears started out catering to a blue collar market and their appliance and tool brands lended themselves to this type of consumer base. Then, in the 1990s, Sears tried to position themselves as an upscale retailer. When they did this, not only did they not attract upscale customers, they alienated their original customer base. Now, not only are they repeating the past, they are repeating a past that failed. Does that make sense to anyone? This is proof the big guys are not immune to making dumb moves.

Their K-mart brand isn't doing any better. Take a look at their marketing. A few years ago their slogan was "Right here, Right now." What the heck does that mean? Are they a convenience store now? The slogan is meaningless and doesn't tell the customer anything at all about the store or brand. More recently they have been using the phrase, "There's smart, then there's K-mart smart." I know I'm not the only one confused by that one. Does that mean only smart people shop at K-mart because I think that's a pretty hard sell. Again the words are meaningless to consumers and do nothing to define their brand.

If the consumer can't figure out what your company is all about, they won't shop there. That is why building a brand that stands for something valuable is so essential. Great warranty, great service, innovative products – or all three! But you must clearly convey that message on a consistent and long term basis so that when your customer sees your logo or advertising they immediately think of value and quality. The most valuable asset, if you want to grow your business, is the value of that brand.

You recall in a previous chapter, I talked about how I would rather buy a dormant business with some brand recognition than start one from scratch? That is because brand value takes so much time, energy and money to build. It is as important, if not more important, than any products you may develop in the future because people will much more readily take a chance on a brand they know and trust even if it is a totally new product.

This is also why you must guard that brand relentlessly. If you start to rest on your laurels or underestimate your customers it will bite you in the butt every time. A good example is the Toyota debacle of 2010. Toyota had, over 33 years, built a brand that was synonymous with quality and value – not an easy thing in the car business. But then they got lazy. There was a problem with the acceleration in some of their cars that was causing accidents and even some deaths. Instead of facing the problem and refocusing on the quality aspect of their business that their brand depended on, they denied everything – for way too long.

Customers, reviewers and analysts crucified the brand destroying the image in just a few months that had taken them 33 years to build. Consumers voted with their dollars and in an already tight car selling market in 2010, Toyota sales crashed and by December 2010 sales were down 37% compared to the previous year. They didn't recover very quickly either as in 2011 month over month sales were down as much as 35% from 2010 in most months depending on the model car.

A brand is hard to build, but easy to destroy, and considering how important it is you can't afford to run the risk of losing it. A strong brand can be a huge boon to growth but only if tended carefully and often. No matter how long you have been in business, or how big your brand eventually is, you can still destroy it in a matter of months if you don't pay very careful attention. An identity crisis can and will kill a brand so you can't allow the fact that your business is getting bigger to be an excuse not to guard that brand with all your might.

Too Many Irons in the Fire

Another way for business to grow is through acquisition and this can be a valid way to expand but only if you do so in the right way. Many businesses expand their market share by buying up or merging with competitors and absorbing their customer base.

That's not to say that it is easy. Trying to bring together two companies even in the exact same business presents a myriad of problems from different corporate cultures to different ideas on marketing or serving the consumers. Just like in a partnership, there is no such thing as a democracy in business and someone has to have the last word. Mergers are famous for ending up as turf battlegrounds rather than for creating a team that works together.

The decision that a business owner has to make is whether to buy out a competitor, merge with them, or simply take over their market. Because of the pitfalls of control, I would favor mergers the least because you want to have control and say over all aspects of the business. Trying to share power or operate by committee will not give you the edge you need to really conquer the market. So I'd slash that one right off the list unless there was some sort of really compelling reason that made it more attractive.

I'm not necessarily thrilled with buying up a competitor unless they have a valuable brand that can be added to yours to strengthen it. If you are just buying them up to get rid of them, you have to really ask yourself if that's worth it because you won't be gaining any type of brand recognition and their customers are going to have to learn about you just as if they were new customers.

If the customers will be just like new customers, then why not just compete harder and win over those customers in the first place? It might not be as fast as buying out the competition but over the long term it can have the same effect – and save you some money. I have seen many products come and go, but those with strong brand recognition and effective marketing outlast their competitors every time.

You must also be careful about adding products because you want to strengthen that brand not dilute it.

It is important to only add products to your line that will be attractive to the same consumer base that you are already marketing to. Again, you don't want to be all things to all people so when you think of developing something new, it should be with that same exact customer in mind in order to get as much help as possible from your existing brand. This is why Oreck vacuums doesn't sell fishing lures!

It may seem a little ridiculous, but companies will often try to expand by adding products that attract an entirely different customer base and this is a recipe for disaster because it is just like starting another business. You have to have two marketing strategies instead of one because the customers are different. If you try to make it all encompassing, you get drivel like the K-mart slogans that mean nothing to anyone.

If you have a strong name and a brand that really stands for something, then you can add products to that brand and have that perception of value carry over to the new product. For example, several years ago, Oreck added an air purifier to our line of products. Oreck was, and is, perceived to make quality products so our customers assumed that the air purifier was of high quality and they were right. The brand stands for something and we stand behind our products. One thing you can't do, however, is add a cheap item to your product line. That will destroy your brand value quicker than anything, so you must focus on upholding the brand. In the end, a brand and a company are made of people and the consumer wants to do business with good people.

You don't have to, nor should you want to, do something totally different to make more money as a small business. You can simply tweak a little here and add a little there and before you know it you are getting the maximum gain for the minimum effort which allows you to put your effort to work attracting even more customers.

CEOs Must Know the Customers

Even after you become successful, it is important to remember and stick to the fundamentals. I recently read about a huge utility company that had hired a new CEO who had previously been in retail. Explain to me how that works! One of the fundamentals of heading a company is to know your customer but as companies grow they tend to get filled with administrators who then hire more administrators. The marketing gets relegated to a department and customers become almost an afterthought. You will never outgrow your customers – but they can outgrow you especially if you lose sight of what is important to them or hire people who have no idea who the customer even is.

No matter how big your company gets, every single person from the receptionist to the CEO needs to understand who pays the bills and that is the customer. One company that was built on this principle and still adheres to it today is Southwest Airlines. They will be the first to tell you that their customers are not the rich and famous. They are not the elite who want to be pampered or who insist on traveling in style. Their customers want to be able to travel with no frills for a great price. That hasn't changed since day one and any employee in their entire company, even four decades after the company first started, can tell you exactly who their customer is. Southwest is very customer centric and their marketing reflects that.

I remember a few years back when other airlines started charging baggage fees and a myriad of other fees. It was really annoying to the consumer who just wanted the price they paid to be the actual price. Southwest jumped on this fact and did a whole series of very funny commercials about the fact that they don't nickel and dime their customers. It was an extremely effective advertising campaign because it was funny and went right to the core of a problem that annoyed people in their potential customer base. In one campaign they hit on the idea that they knew their customers, treated them right and had a great sense of humor. That is what made it effective. It is not rocket science, but it is well thought out advertising with their customers uppermost in their minds.

Cash is Still King

As you become more successful you can offer terms to customers that will increase your sales. You may offer your product for three payments of $79 rather than one of $199. It is a little counter intuitive to some to understand why people would agree to pay so much more for a product but it is a fact of consumer behavior that we want things now; we just don't always have the cash on hand. Nothing bears this out like the success of the rent to own business. They offer furniture, appliances and things like televisions and computers for a low weekly amount and no credit check. Of course you end up paying at least two to three times what the item is worth but it is still attractive to many. People will tell you that they can't afford a $100 per month payment, but they can afford $25 per week. It may sound like the same thing, but it is not to them.

Many consumers have this incremental mindset. They consider a small amount of money discretionary, but once the dollar amount of each payment climbs they feel like they can't afford it or that the money should go to something more important. Car dealers have known this for years and now the most frequent question they ask when someone walks into the dealership is "What payment can you afford?" Then they simply fit the vehicle to the payment. That may mean the person ends up with a seven year loan at 10%, but they don't care because in their minds they can 'afford' the payment.

It is important to understand this mindset because as an entrepreneur, while it can be a great way to increase business, it can work against you too. When you think about offering terms to anyone, it is easy to think you can afford to do that. But you have to understand how this new strategy affects inventory and cash flow. There is no way on earth I'd ever advise a new entrepreneur to offer terms simply because most just aren't stable enough. You just can't offer terms and carry receivables while remaining healthy as a business. First, you must get a very solid financial base of sales going. Even then, offering terms to customers too soon can get you in hot water very quickly and force you to consider options (like taking on partners or investors) that may hurt you down the road.

As you grow, you may consider offering terms but only on a limited basis at first. You want to develop good data to work with to estimate what making a term offer to a larger segment of the market will do to your cash flow and overall company performance. You don't want to get this wrong or guess at it because it is your business on the line.

Cash is still king at every stage of business and keeping good cash reserves no matter what expansion route you pursue will allow you to make a misstep or two without it costing you your entire business. As you start to expand the most important thing is to go slowly and evaluate constantly. The last thing you ever want to be is one of those companies that grew itself to death!

**David Oreck 2005 in his
open cockpit Waco**

David Oreck

Oreck Wisdom:

You've got a business...
Mind it.

David Oreck

10

SUCCESS ON YOUR OWN TERMS

David Oreck

Chapter 10
Success on Your Own Terms

There is an old Sinatra tune called "I Did it My Way" and that is how I feel about my own success in business. Every person's experience will be different but the key principles I've outlined in this book never change. It doesn't matter if you are making yo-yos or building yachts, it's still these same ideas that will make you successful or, if ignored, cause your business to fade into oblivion. Being small is not a crime and gives you wonderful advantages so don't underestimate your ability to not only compete with the big boys, but be successful at it.

Many people reading this book will be small business people as they will relate the most to my message and story of the success of Oreck vacuums. You may think you've heard this before or that I have spent a lot of time repeating myself. Both of those thoughts are correct and the reason is that so many business people don't get the simple things right. If you aren't as successful as you want to be and you think this book won't help you, read it again – and keep doing so until you fully grasp the reality that the simple ideas are the easiest to mess up.

Even executives of multinational corporations have something to learn because sitting in a big office doesn't give you the knowledge base to correctly choose what to do when things aren't going well. We all know the cyclical nature of business and large businesses are even more vulnerable to making the mistakes I've outlined than small ones. Why? Because there is more at stake and many executives are so concerned with protecting their backside they don't even pretend to fix the problems. Often they have such distance from the customers that they have no clue how to save the business when those customers start to flee. Big companies don't make little missteps; they fall hard. But it doesn't have to be that way if they get back to the basics that got that company and that brand to the top in the first place. Every big business was once a small business and it would serve them well to remember that.

My business experience has spanned almost 70 years and over that time I've actually only had two jobs, my job with RCA and working for myself at Oreck Corp. I was at RCA for 17 years.

I started at the bottom and ended up the general sales manager running all the sales of the company where we represented some of the biggest brands of the day including RCA, Whirlpool, and International Harvester as exclusive wholesaler in New York. I learned much during those years and I also know that though these brands were big and powerful, many of them are out of business now as are many of the department stores that carried those goods.

This illustrates the biggest truth in business and that is that the sales environment is always changing and always will. The exciting part is to know that there will always be a place for the small business that can quickly and easily shift as customer tastes and preferences shift. That was true of my second job building and running Oreck Inc.

Over 40 years, we built a brand based on value and were very successful. But the only real constant is change and if you are willing to accept that fact as an entrepreneur, and persist, you will see the opportunities as they arise and be able to make a place for yourself and your brand.

From Dust to Diamonds
Prioritizing the Steps

This book is meant to give you some practical and sound advice that you can start to use immediately in your business and to that end, I've decided to give you a final playbook. I've talked about many key concepts such as knowing your customer, understanding how to market effectively and many others. When I talk about these to business owners, invariably they want to know how to rank the concepts in order of most important or what they should focus on first. While there is some variance depending on the type of business and circumstance, I will explain which concepts I believe to be the most important.

The National Federation of Independent Business' Education Foundation (NFIB) estimates that over the lifetime of a business, 39% are profitable, 30% break even, and 30% lose money, with 1% falling in the "unable to determine" category. What that says to me is that more than 60% of small businesses have no idea who their customer is or how to market to them. Even of the ones that do turn a profit, I would wager that they are not near as profitable as they could be by fully understanding what motivates their customers to buy.

When you decide to go into business, the odds are long - not because it is hard, but because most owners have preconceived ideas about how it 'should' be. These ideas have come from business schools, books, and the supposed wisdom spouted on many a business news program.

This information often glosses over identifying the customer and focuses instead on trying to shove sales down people's throats. There is an old joke I love that illustrates this idea.

A fellow in New York City approached a man in the Bronx who lived in an apartment on the third floor.

The fellow said, "I have an elephant for sale, only $2,000."

The man says, "That sounds pretty cheap, but I don't need the elephant. I live on the third floor and I couldn't possibly have him."

"But listen, this isn't just some ordinary elephant. It can sing and dance so you could rent him out for birthday parties for children."

The man says, "That sounds fine, but after all I live on the third floor. I couldn't just leave him out on the street in New York and I couldn't bring him into the apartment. So, you see, I just couldn't use him."

The fellow says, "I'll tell you what I'll do. I let you have two elephants for $2,000."

The man says, "Well, now you're talking!"

This joke always makes me smile because it illustrates exactly how many businesses market to, and treat, their customers. They don't care about any feedback they receive or meeting the customer's needs or even who that customer is, they just want to sell, sell, SELL! What they get is short term results but a long term disaster. Often they don't even get much short term so it is a disaster all the way around.

I have repeatedly talked about knowing your customer and this one concept is so important that it overshadows every other important idea I've presented. How can you market if you don't know who you are marketing to? How can you bring new products to the marketplace if you don't know who they will be most suited to? How can you grow a business if you don't know which customers will support that growth?

Every single thing you ever do as a business comes back to that one point – know thy customer. By specifically and completely identifying your customer, you give yourself the right place to start to succeed.

This identification is not just sitting and thinking about who your product or service might be good for, it is about finding that person most likely to buy right now, today and that's a big difference. Your market is never 'everyone' – nor should it be. You can't afford to spend too much time and energy on the guy that might buy a year from now; you could be out of business by then. Focus on the person who needs what you have to offer today and then create your marketing to close the deal for that person, not everyone else. Failure to specifically focus on the most likely customer is a grave mistake and has sunk many businesses before they even really got off the ground.

The second most critical concept is the absolute control of your distribution. I very much encourage people starting in business to sell direct. Selling direct to the end user, not to a distributor who in turn redistributes or resells that product gives you ultimate control. If it is in any way feasible for your type of business to sell direct, then it is imperative that you do so as it will be a key component of long term success.

You control your pricing, your production and most importantly how and when you get paid. I would even go so far as to say forget about retailers like Wal-Mart. Forget about 'em. Sell direct and do not offer terms. Cash is your friend. Encourage your customers to use credit cards; the credit card companies can offer credit and assume that risk but you don't have to.

Marketing is one of the most misused and least understood concepts in business today. Marketing isn't just advertising, it is building your brand and winning over the hearts and minds of your customers. Then it is about keeping them. You must differentiate your product or service from everyone else out there on the market and then you have to get that message to customers. You have to find what makes you unique and why the customer would favor you over others. You will recall in the marketing chapter I told you to pick a few key points – like maybe two or three and work with those relentlessly. You may have a list of 15 great things about your business, but you have to narrow it down and specifically choose the ones that speak the most to your target market. You want to bring customers to you so that you have the chance to educate them on the value you offer over others.

I believe in advertising. Advertising is education. It is not something you do if you have extra money and it is certainly not something you cut back on when times are hard. That's like being all alone in the desert and pouring out the only water you have – it spells doom. Advertise, advertise, advertise. But where, what, and how you advertise are crucial questions and the way you figure that out is to go back to number one, which is know your customer. Where they live, what they buy and how they behave.

This allows you to choose media that targets them specifically. And of course test, test, test to narrow down the type of ad they respond to and in what format. This ties in directly to brand building – advertising and branding are linked together like twin sisters. As you advertise you are also building your brand and educating your customers on what your company stands for and this never stops as long as you are in business.

Building a brand is a slow process and it requires long term consistent messaging and tweaking.

I think this aspect is more difficult today than it has ever been. The reason being that brand building years ago from the early time of TV was simpler in that if you wanted to advertise on TV, for example, you had only three networks you could choose to advertise on. You knew that running an ad on just one of them would capture roughly one third of the audience. Today, there are hundreds of TV stations, thousands of radio stations and there is no one network or even group of networks that attracts one third of the American audience in any media form.

There are an unlimited number of places today where the customer's eyes and ears could go without seeing your ad. They can go to the cable television, radio stations and even their computer screens. You have to work hard at building your brand for a long time before it starts to work for you and then you have to do everything you can to protect and support it.

You have to be creative to compete. This means that you have to dare to be different and think outside the norm. You can't just hop into the race and then copy what the big guys are doing. Remember that is like bringing a knife to a gun fight because you can't fight the bully on his own turf.

This was a big consideration with my company because lets' face it, vacuums aren't anything new. I had to find a way to get mine to stand out and I chose the fact that it was lightweight. This was during a time when heft was synonymous with value and performance so we had an uphill battle.

But we were creative and once we hit upon the idea combining lightweight with the perception of commercial quality (by using the picture of a hotel maid holding the vacuum over her head) customers responded. We also refused to play the one-upmanship game when tools on board became all the rage. Just because a competitor jumps one way doesn't mean you follow. We didn't and instead offered a whole additional lightweight canister vacuum. Again, customers responded. Of course if we'd consulted a business 'expert' at the time they would have said we were crazy and doomed to fail – but they would have been wrong. Creativity can get you a long way.

At the very beginning of this book I talked about needing a widget – the type of widget is largely unimportant. By this I meant that you can choose any type of business or product, you don't have to choose something completely revolutionary.

In fact, by choosing a more ordinary item that people already know they need and changing it slightly you benefit because you don't have to take the extra step of convincing customers they need it. Do you need to convince customers that they need clean carpet? Or a car to drive? Or clothes to wear? Or food to eat? Of course not, so while entering these categories may pit you against some of the largest corporations around, you can quickly find a specific niche that they aren't filling and that becomes your domain.

For example, how often do you hear about (or eat at) a family owned restaurant that has been in business 50, 60 or even 70 years through several generations? It is not because they beat out the big fast food chains, it is because they offer something very specific that customers can only get in that one business and they will loyally come back year after year and generation after generation. The product itself doesn't matter, but the ability to market, and then offer great service to your customers, does. Here again, this comes back to the #1 concept I feel you must understand – know your customer.

The very last consideration for any business is the price of their product or service. I'm not saying to ignore this point, just understand that price is the least important factor in getting people to buy. I always tell business owners that they need a widget that is a considered purchase – in other words toward the upper end of the pricing range rather than the cheapest.

You will never win competing on price and it is important to build into the price of your product the time, energy and advertising it will take to educate those customers on the value you are offering. That is why using middle men or retailers to get your product out there may not be the best idea. They end up controlling the price and then you never have the money to really build your brand into a force to be reckoned with.

Don't fall into the trap of focusing your advertising on price or thinking that you have to be cheap to grow your business. You don't want every customer, you want the right customers. The ones who want quality and are willing to pay for it – and that is more people than you think.

If you give them a unique or unusual experience in quality or service or anything else, they feel they got a good deal no matter what the price or product is. For example, almost every time a conversation with a BMW owner takes place, they immediately start telling you how valuable their car is – not necessarily what they paid, but why this particular machine is the ultimate driving machine.

Now does it get you from place to place the same as a used Chevy? You bet, but BMW has spent many years and many dollars educating their customers about quality and performance of their uniquely engineered cars to the point that the consumers they are targeting will pay whatever the price is to own one. In fact, if a new BMW owner even mentions how much they paid it is to prove to you what a great deal they got!

This is exactly the concept you want to convey with your product. Price is only a measure of the perception of value that you have created and the more value you can inject, the higher the price should be. Don't be afraid to target a small group of the right customers and don't under price yourself and think you are playing it safe. I've seen business owners create a tremendous amount of value for a product, but then under price it to the point that people think that value is worthless or that their ads are not being truthful. You can't tell people you have the best performing car on the road that was ever built and then price it at $10,000. It doesn't make sense.

You must step up your pricing each time you add value – otherwise it feels like you are adding a second elephant for free! People know when a sales pitch is over the top and this turns them off.

Tell them what is so great about your product or service, price it accordingly and then over deliver. Rather than being suspicious or turned off, they will be thrilled and long term customer loyalty is vital to your success.

The Last Word

I will tell you that today I'm neck deep in several other businesses that I've created since I sold the vacuum business and I love it. It keeps me challenged and every single day I learn something new and valuable about customer behavior. I'd like to say at this point that I'm never shocked by what motives customers but in reality sometimes it shocks the hell out of me! It is that kind of discovery that makes business such a challenge and hey, if it was easy everyone would do it and be a millionaire to boot!

I've always heard that anything worth doing is going to be hard and that's a good thing. It is those hard lessons that have taught me the most and though circumstances may be trying at times, they will help you as well. If you think you have the right stuff, don't let anyone dissuade you from what you want.

You can learn much from other experienced entrepreneurs and as long as you are open to those lessons, you can shorten your learning curve and increase your profitability.

There is no great secret to business other than understanding the basic ideas I've conveyed here. Now it is up to you and all I can tell you is to work hard, market hard and build a business that knows its customer and puts them first.

David Oreck

Oreck Wisdom:

Don't ask for my opinion,
unless you plan to take it.
Otherwise you're just wasting my time
and yours.

David Oreck

David and Jan Oreck 2007

David Oreck is an American entrepreneur and patriot. He served as a pilot in World War II, and then returned to begin a career in sales in New York City, far away from his Midwest roots.

After almost two decades of sales and marketing experience in the corporate world, Oreck struck out on his own and founded the Oreck company. He then made it a household name.

Oreck's success came through a clear and unique understanding of how to market a small business and he shares that knowledge with lecture audiences and entrepreneurs nationwide.

Not one to rest on his laurels, since selling Oreck Inc. in the 1990s, David Oreck now runs several entrepreneurial start ups and manages them from his offices in New Orleans.

David Oreck

CPSIA information can be obtained at www.ICGtesting.com
Printed in the USA
BVOW041810220513

321356BV00001B/2/P